Compassionate Dialogue
JOURNEY

Copyright © 2024 Nancy A. Dome

All rights reserved. No part of this book may be used or reproduced in any manner whatsoever without prior written consent of the author, except as provided by the United States of America copyright law.

Published by Fire Horse Rising LLC, Hot Springs, MT 59845

Fire Horse Rising LLC is a registered trademark.

ISBN: 979-8-218-42124-3

This publication is designed to provide accurate and authoritative information with regard to the subject matter covered. It is sold with the understanding that the publisher is not engaged in rendering legal, accounting, or other professional advice. If legal advice or other expert assistance is required, the services of a competent professional should be sought.

Most Fire Horse Rising LLC titles are available at special quantity discounts for bulk purchases for sales promotions, premiums, fundraising, and educational use. Special versions or book excerpts can also be created to fit specific needs.

For more information, please write:

Fire Horse Rising LLC
PO Box 676
Hot Springs, Montana 59845

Compassionate Dialogue JOURNEY

**The Compassionate Dialogue Journey:
A Workbook for Growth and Self-Discovery**

By Nancy A. Dome, Ed.D

The Compassionate Dialogue Framework through the RIR Protocol
(Recognize It! Interrupt It! Repair It!) is copyrighted by EpochEducation.com © 2021

Fire Horse Rising LLC
Hot Springs, Montana

To anyone who has ever struggled to find the right words,
who wants to connect but isn't sure how,
who believes this world can be better
. . . and who wants to be part of making it so.
This book is for you.

CONTENTS

Foreword 13

Before We Begin 15
    The Basics 16
        Tips for Success 19
        The Three Spheres of Impact 21
        Terms to Remember 21
    What's Next? 26

Module 1: What is Compassionate Dialogue, and Why Am I On This Journey? 29
    A Closer Look at Compassionate Dialogue 29
    The Good Person/Bad Person Binary 32
    Tone and Body Language 33
        Activity: Find Your Equity Avatar 34
    Practice & Implementation 38

Module 2: Understanding the RIR Protocol 41
    Recognize 42
        The Physical, Mental, and Emotional Process of Recognizing ... 43
    Interrupt 44
        Activity: My "Why" For Interrupting 46

 How To Interrupt..47

Repair 49
 How to Repair..50

Receiving the Protocol 52
 Activity: Receiving the Protocol 53

Putting It All Together..53

What's Next? 55

Module 3: My Intrapersonal Journey and The RIR 57

Your Feeling Journey 58
 Activity: My Racial Experience 58
 Activity: My Identity Chart 61

Your Intrapersonal Recognize, Examined 63

Fixed and Growth Mindset: A Deeper Dive 65

"Non-Ness" and Unconscious Bias 66

The Cycle of Inference..68

Your Intrapersonal Interrupt, Examined 71
 Activity: Exploring Your Own Unconscious Language and Bias (Part 1)..72

Your Intrapersonal Repair, Examined 73
 Activity: Exploring Your Own Unconscious Language and Bias (Part 2)..73

Putting "The Feeling Journey" All Together 74

What's Next? 75

Module 4: My Interpersonal Journey and The RIR 77

Your Interpersonal Recognize, Examined 78

The Cycle of Inference: Interpersonal 79

Activity: Assess Your Relationship with the Cycle of Inference 83

Your Interpersonal Interrupt, Examined 83

Activity: Practice, Practice, Practice 88

Your Interpersonal Repair, Examined 90

Activity: Reflecting on the Big Picture 91

What's Next? 93

Module 5: My Organizational Journey and The RIR 95

Your Organizational Recognize, Examined 97

Mirrors, Windows, and Sliding Glass Doors 98

Your Organizational Interrupt, Examined 100

Activity (Option 1): Equity Walk Through Tool—How Inclusive Is Your Brand/Company? 100

Activity (Option 2): Equity Audit—How Inclusive Is Your Classroom? 102

Review and Refine Your Approach 103

Your Organizational Repair, Examined 104

Activity: Walking Your Organization Through The RIR 105

What's Next? 107

Module 6: What's Next? Compassionate Dialogue and RIR Application and Practice 109

Bringing It All Together: Receiving the Protocol 112

Activity: My Compassionate Dialogue Journey Reflection and Portfolio ... 114

Your Commitment Statement, Revisited 115

Before You Go 117

Resources 119

Acknowledgments 135

About the Author 137

FOREWORD

To quote my friend Dr. Nancy Dome: "This will feel like soul work because it's supposed to." With those words, Dr. Dome captures the true power and joy of this book. Her tireless dedication to promoting equity, inclusion, and justice has inspired countless individuals—including me—to rise up and take action towards creating a more understanding and considerate world.

Given the incredible impact she has had on my own life, it was a tremendous honor when she asked me to write the foreword for this workbook, which celebrates not only her life, but also her powerful work around issues of diversity and race. Conversations about these topics can be challenging and uncomfortable, yet they are more essential than ever in our society.

In this workbook and throughout her life, Nancy continually brings us back to one truth: when the stakes are high and emotions run strong, we have three choices. We can avoid a critical conversation and suffer the consequences later (and make no mistake: there will be consequences, both to ourselves and to those around us). We can handle the conversation poorly and suffer the consequences of doing so in the present moment. Or, we can apply the lessons and strategies in this workbook and experience an immediate and profound impact on our relationships, career, happiness, and future.

In a world where differences in opinion and perspective seem to divide us more than ever before, this work of connecting with each other, of being in community—this work that we call diversity, equity, and inclusion—might feel daunting and never-ending. But it doesn't have to be, and that's what Nancy so brilliantly conveys in this workbook. Through real-life examples, practical techniques, and insightful reflections, Nancy illuminates the power of listening, asking questions, creating connections, and promoting understanding. In doing so, she teaches us the art of engaging in Compassionate Dialogue™, which, at its heart, is really a simple, heartfelt conversation that leaves space for us and the other person to stand in the truth of our shared humanity.

This is a timely contribution to the ongoing effort for belonging in our world, and I truly believe it will inspire all who read it to engage in the impactful conversations that are so crucial to creating a more compassionate and diverse society, while simultaneously providing the tools necessary to navigate these conversations with empathy and respect.

There is no time better than now to lean into this work. The world we live in has left so many of us reeling, desperate to find a way to end the senseless suffering and hatred that seems to permeate every level of society. And yet, in the midst of the suffering, there's hope: the hope that if we could just understand each other better, we could and would get along better.

Nancy's workbook makes this hope seem achievable. It makes it attainable. It makes it practical. It makes it WORK! By embracing its lessons, we learn to become part of the group tapestry that makes the phrase "liberty and justice for all" ring true.

This workbook is a testament to the transformative force that education, activism, and empathy can have on our lives and communities. It is my sincerest hope that this book not only honors my friend's life and legacy, but also serves as a call to action for us all to continue working towards a more just and equitable world, while inspiring readers to discover the profound sense of peace and compassion that lies within us all.

– With Love, Amikaeyla Gaston
Founder, The International Cultural Arts and Healing Sciences Institute (ICAHSI)
Co-Executive Director, World Trust

Before We Begin

"We can communicate in a way that inspires growth."

When I started this work over twenty years ago, I was in a very different place than I am now: though my goal was the same, I was sometimes direct (the Sagittarius coming out in me, I know) to the point of ineffectiveness. That's changed, but it is an example of a larger point: when I think of all the areas I've grown in since I began this journey, I know I've made a lot of mistakes. . . but I've also learned a lot and have fundamentally changed for the better. While my commitment to my values has remained unchanged, I've become softer, more vulnerable, and more willing to take risks. This didn't happen overnight. In fact, it's still happening right now, at this moment. Why? Because the work we're trying to accomplish personally and professionally is truly a journey, not a destination. Over the years, I've learned that if my goal is to build connection, I have to figure out a way to build bridges with people with whom I don't feel like I have a lot in common. So, too, will you.

My invitation to you as you move through this workbook is to keep an open heart and an open mind. Try to remove blame, for yourself and others. We are all going to make mistakes in life; that is how we grow. Sometimes, adversity can be a teacher. How do we feel something that might not be gracious and still move forward, in our own growth and our growth with one another? That's what I'm hoping to offer you from this Compassionate Dialogue Journey.

We are having this Compassionate Dialogue conversation for ourselves, certainly, and we'll discuss how using it is a form of self-care. In the bigger picture, though, I want you to understand that **Compassionate Dialogue is a pathway to creating belonging, equity, and justice because how we think and act impacts the climates and cultures we create. The ultimate goal, then, is to create climates and cultures where people can be who they are—for ourselves and for everyone.**

Before we start, though, let's talk a little bit about how we got here in the first place. In

2021, I wrote a book called *Let's Talk About Race (and Other Hard Things): A Framework for Having Conversations That Build Bridges, Strengthen Relationships, and Set Clear Boundaries*. In it, I shared strategies for handling uncomfortable situations like the ones I alluded to above. Primary among those strategies is the RIR Protocol™, a component of Compassionate Dialogue®.

The RIR—which stands for Recognize, Interrupt, Repair—shows us there is another way . . . a better way. It, like Compassionate Dialogue itself, teaches a more humane, compassionate way to engage, disagree, heal, grow, and move forward. So often, we get stuck in our fear—fear of not saying the right thing, fear of retaliation, fear of not having the right information, fear of not knowing enough, or fear of not having the right to speak on a topic. All these barriers get in the way of caring for ourselves and effectively engaging with one another. I've spent many years teaching people like you how to remove those barriers by proposing a new way to approach these conversations—a way that says you don't have to have all the answers. Instead, you simply have to self—reflect, check in, ask questions, and commit to staying engaged.

If you've picked up this book, you've already accepted an invitation to grow. Let's take a closer look at what comes next.

The Basics

Compassionate Dialogue and the RIR Protocol go beyond the warm and fuzzy idea of just communicating with empathy. They give us the tools to face uncomfortable situations, deepen our connections to ourselves and others, and solve problems in a way that helps us move forward . . . not stay stuck.

Why is this important? Because we all have problems. Challenges and conflict—internal, external, or some combination of the two—arise every day. They are simply part of the human experience. That internal piece, the voice in our head and our relationship to it, is often the first and most important place to start.

That voice that says, *This person is attacking me and trying to hurt me, and I'm not going to let him so put your defenses up and attack back!* [Fight]

Or, *This person is too aggressive and will not listen to me. I'm uncomfortable and possibly unsafe, so I need to get out of here as soon as possible!* [Flight]

Or, *I cannot believe she just said what she said. I am shocked but have no idea what to do or say . . . so I'm not going to do or say anything.* [Freeze]

Or, *I don't agree with what they're saying, but I need a way to get out of this interaction quickly and don't want things to get too uncomfortable. I will just nod in false agreement to get this over with so we can change the subject.* [Fawn]

Or, *I think I should say something but don't know what to say, so I'm just going to go along with the crowd on this one, though I might feel guilty about that later.* [Flock]

There is no one right way to handle these thoughts and the situations that caused or resulted in them. The good news is that you don't have to have all the answers. (As we know, there's usually more than one, anyway.) Instead, what we need to do is self-reflect, ask questions, and stay engaged. This works because another part of the human experience is having the capacity to grow and change. We are not powerless or doomed to respond to problems in the same way forever. Rather, there is a way to have a more intentional and gentle relationship with how we move through the world as individuals.

That's why I invite you to think about the RIR Protocol, and Compassionate Dialogue on the whole, as a form of not only self-regulation, but also self-care.

What if you could resolve problems or uncomfortable situations in ways that are meaningful and productive? What if you could learn from them, and learn more about yourself in the process? What if, instead of beating yourself up after the fact or not getting the result you wanted in the moment, you could connect more deeply or set better boundaries? What if doing all these things created a pathway to more equity in our world and more communities of belonging for us all?

The RIR Protocol does this. It says: "I can use this tool to regulate myself, my choice of words, and how I choose to engage. Others don't control my feelings or my actions. I am open to making mistakes, giving grace to myself and others, and trying my best to stay engaged each and every day. When I do that, I not only see better outcomes and feel more comfortable solving problems, but I can take better care of myself in the process."

It sounds transformative because it is. And you can have it for yourself.

On this journey, you will learn how to use the protocol to develop skills for self-reflection and effective communication that will ultimately provide a common language for examining bigger issues in ourselves, our relationships, and our world.

Specifically, be prepared to:

Overcome the judgments you may not even know you have. We all have them. We all act out of them. But we don't always know when we're doing it. What you think is helpful might be hurtful. My hope is that this journey will enlighten you because if you want to make changes on the outside, you have to start on the inside. This does not mean we won't continue to have judgment, as it is near impossible not to. What it does mean, though, is that we do not let it drive us. That we refrain from accepting it as fact until we have inquired to be sure one way or the other using the protocol.

Participate in professional and personal development that will transform your thinking and readiness to be a leader for Compassionate Dialogue. You will master the ability to lead productive conversations that don't devolve into destructive arguments. You will acquire and sharpen some of the most important leadership skills—resolving conflicts, practicing self-awareness, opening hearts, and deepening our compassion for one another.

Recognize, Interrupt and Repair your own unconscious bias. Sustainable change starts from the inside out, and leading with Compassionate Dialogue means taking responsibility for our own growth. We all have issues we need to resolve, and we all make judgments. We don't, though, always know when they are guiding our thoughts and actions. That's why the "Recognize" piece of The RIR Protocol is so important.

However, I understand not everyone is able to identify feelings in the same way. We all have a different relationship to our emotions and how we identify and process them. That's why you'll find a tool we call the Feelings Wheel, which you'll be seeing in many of our other modules, too. There are two ways to use it: you can go from the outside in (nuanced emotions to core emotions) or inside out (core emotions to nuanced emotions). Start at whichever feels most intuitive. There is value in either approach, as understanding both core and ancillary emotions are pathways to help you get down to their root causes quicker.

We support your growth in this area so you can support your own growth and that of others.

At the end of our time together, you can expect to be able to utilize the RIR Protocol in your everyday life—internally in how you process situations, thoughts, and feelings; in conversations with friends or family; and in meetings at work or other systems-oriented settings.

Tips for Success

I invite you to embark upon this journey with an open mind and open heart. **This will feel like soul work because it's supposed to.** And while you'll eventually reach the end of the exercises, I hope you'll continue to incorporate what you learned from them in your everyday life. There is no finish line here; success looks like practice and commitment.

At the end of the day, using the protocol helps develop skills for self-reflection, effective communication, and provides a common language for examining systemic equity-related issues that exist in our groups and organizations.

It sounds great, right? **Along this journey, we'll take the RIR Protocol and Compassionate Dialogue from the conceptual to the actionable and experiential in a way that is structured around targeted activities designed specifically for implementation and reflection.**

A *whole lot* of reflection.

For this reason, to complete this workbook, you'll need a place to compile your thoughts as we move through this journey together. **Before you move forward, designate a notebook or document on your computer—whatever feels comfortable—in which you will answer the prompts and reflection questions that are core to this workbook.**

It's important to:

- **Keep your work in one place.** This will allow you to refer to prior responses if need be. Ultimately, it will also give you a more holistic view of your evolution and progress.
- **Check judgment at the door.** As a well-intentioned person, you probably care deeply about saying the right thing. There is no single "right thing" to say for any of the questions or prompts in this book. Try not to judge your answers as you write them and instead meet yourself where you truly are. That's how true progress starts.
- **Consider working with a group or partner.** You can certainly complete the exercises in this workbook on your own, and everything you need to do just that is included in these pages. However, like most journeys, this one can be more rewarding and effective if you take it with a growth-minded person or a group you trust. If you choose this route, set aside designated time to check in with your partner(s), share responses that you're comfortable sharing, and discuss takeaways and reflections.
- **Take the time you need.** Though how you structure your self-guided journey is ultimately up to you, we recommend being prepared to dedicate roughly two to three hours a week to this practice.
- **Take advantage of the activities and journaling prompts.** Throughout this book, you'll see two specific types of opportunities to engage more with the concepts. In the activities, you'll find fodder for deep thought and exploratory actions to expand your practice. The journaling prompts—signaled with ✑ —offer extra opportunities to pick up your pen (or turn on your computer, or use your

workbook vehicle of choice for this work) and get what's in your head out into your physical space. These elements have been specifically designed to help you internalize this work and get the most from your practice. Please use them.

The Three Spheres of Impact

The focus of this work is threefold: intrapersonal (with yourself), interpersonal (with others), and organizational (within systems, groups, or structures).

What's the difference? And what does this mean practically? The following chart provides sample applications.

 Intrapersonal
 Interpersonal
 Organizational

- Stuck on a tough decision.
- Need movement to act.
- Challenge a belief.

- Disagreement with colleague.
- Encounter with stranger.
- Intervention with child.
- Interacting with family members.
- Conflict with a friend.

- Policy and procedure review.
- Hiring and promotion access.
- Brand assessment.
- Addressing internal power dynamics.

As you can see, Intrapersonal RIR is for use within your own mind and spirit. Interpersonal RIR is for situations involving others, such as resolving conflicts with friends or family. Organizational RIR is for systems-level work, such as in your workplace or group. After examining the differences among the three spheres, consider adding your own. For example, if you're in education, you might add "curriculum review" or "disproportionate discipline" to the Organizational column.

Terms to Remember

Before we dive in, let's define some key terms and concepts. You may choose to bookmark this page to reference throughout your Compassionate Dialogue Journey.

Compassionate Dialogue: Epoch Education's Compassionate Dialogue is a way to resolve a problem or find a solution through connection and showing empathy for others and ourselves. It is a more humane, kind, and productive way to engage, disagree, heal, grow, solve problems, and move forward.

RIR: The Epoch Education RIR Protocol is a simple 3-step framework [*Recognize, Interrupt, Repair*] proven to help tough conversations go beyond conflict and invite understanding, empathy, and connection. **The RIR Protocol is the foundation of the Compassionate Dialogue Journey.** Whether you're addressing complex topics like issues of race, gender, disability, the LGBTQ+ community, and educational equality, or navigating simpler terrain, the RIR Protocol gives you a roadmap for constructive conversations that you can use in any situation. It is designed to create a culture where people appreciate each other's differences and give each other the freedom to be their best.

Intersectionality: Kimberlé Crenshaw introduced the theory of intersectionality, the idea that when it comes to thinking about how inequalities persist—categories like gender, race, and class—are best understood as overlapping and mutually constitutive rather than isolated and distinct. By definition, it is the complex, cumulative way in which the effects of multiple forms of discrimination (such as racism, sexism, and classism) combine, overlap, or intersect especially in the experiences of marginalized individuals or groups.

Culture: Culture is defined as the traits and beliefs shared by a group of people united by religion, race, or social elements. In other words, culture is truly about your lived experiences, and those can be varied. It's true that there is a Black culture, a surfer culture, a southern culture, and so on, but it's not true that we must pick one of those boxes only. For example, I am a Black woman who grew up in West Hollywood, so my cultural experience will be different from that of a Black woman who grew up in the south. Our surroundings and experiences—i.e., our culture(s)—impact how we see, experience, and move through the world around us.

Equality: At its most basic level, equality is when everyone gets the same thing. The idea is admirable, and I understand that the goal of equality as a social practice is deeply rooted in good intentions. However, ultimately, what we want is for everyone to get what they need, not necessarily the exact same. Take, for example, standards in the classroom. Some students will fall far below the standard, some students will be close to the standard, and some students will be above the standard. When we teach each of those students in the same way, that is equality. *Equality says, "I am focused on the big picture."* The problem is that they will not all benefit in the same way from that practice because they are in *different* places. Therefore, it would be better to give each what they need to excel, which likely looks different for each student. That is where our next key term comes in.

Equity: Whereas equality is giving everyone the same thing, equity is giving everyone what they need. It is teaching each student in that classroom we just discussed in the way that will help them hit or surpass that standard. Whereas equality is all about the big picture, the idea of differentiation is core to the concept of equity. People want to be seen, and though it takes more work, the payoff is often greater. *Equity says, "I see you."*

Equality	Equity	Justice

The assumption is that everyone benefits from the same supports. This is equal treatment.	Everyone gets the supports they need, thus producing equity.	All three can see the game without supports or accommodations because the cause(s) of inequity were addressed. The systemic barrier has been removed.

Justice: Justice unpacks and addresses the root causes of a lack of equity in the first place. If the students below the standard in our classroom example are struggling, justice calls for us to look at why that is, not just what we can do to fix it for now. Of course, there certainly is value in "fixing it for now." When someone is hurt, you stop the bleeding before you try to diagnose what went wrong. Justice, however, doesn't stop there. Justice says, *"I understand the root cause, and I'm going to fix it."*

Non-ness: Non-ness is the outcome of conscious or unconscious deficit biases or beliefs about each other or ourselves. It shows up as: exclusion, invisibility, dehumanization, a single narrative, devaluing, stereotyping, and more. Specifically, non-ness looks at how we use language to marginalize individuals and groups through nuanced, deficit— focused language. It is, for example, our habit of identifying people by what they are not rather than by what they are or judging them against a perceived norm (like "non-white" or "non-English speaker") rather than language that honors who they are ("Chinese" or "second language learner").

Tone policing: Tone policing is a conversational tactic that dismisses the ideas being communicated when they are perceived to be delivered in an angry, frustrated, sad, fearful or otherwise emotionally-charged manner. It becomes a way to detour a conversation from the issue and focus more on communication styles, which can be inherently biased depending on who is speaking. For example, people of color often find that their voices are minimized because they are perceived to be "angry" or "aggressive."

Feelings: You might be thinking, "Feelings? I know what those are. Why do I need that word defined?" The answer is that sometimes, what we think is a feeling is actually a judgment. We all judge unconsciously; it's impossible not to. But what we do next—the feeling or emotion we then need to process within ourselves—is where the following Feelings Wheel comes into play. There are big feelings (sad, angry, happy, etc.) that we often use as blanket terms for a host of more specific emotions. The Feelings Wheel helps provide language to reach that level of specificity, which strengthens our relationship with the "Recognize" part of The RIR Protocol. In short, **if your "Recognize" doesn't fall on this wheel (or close to it), it's likely not a feeling and is a sign you need to dig deeper.**

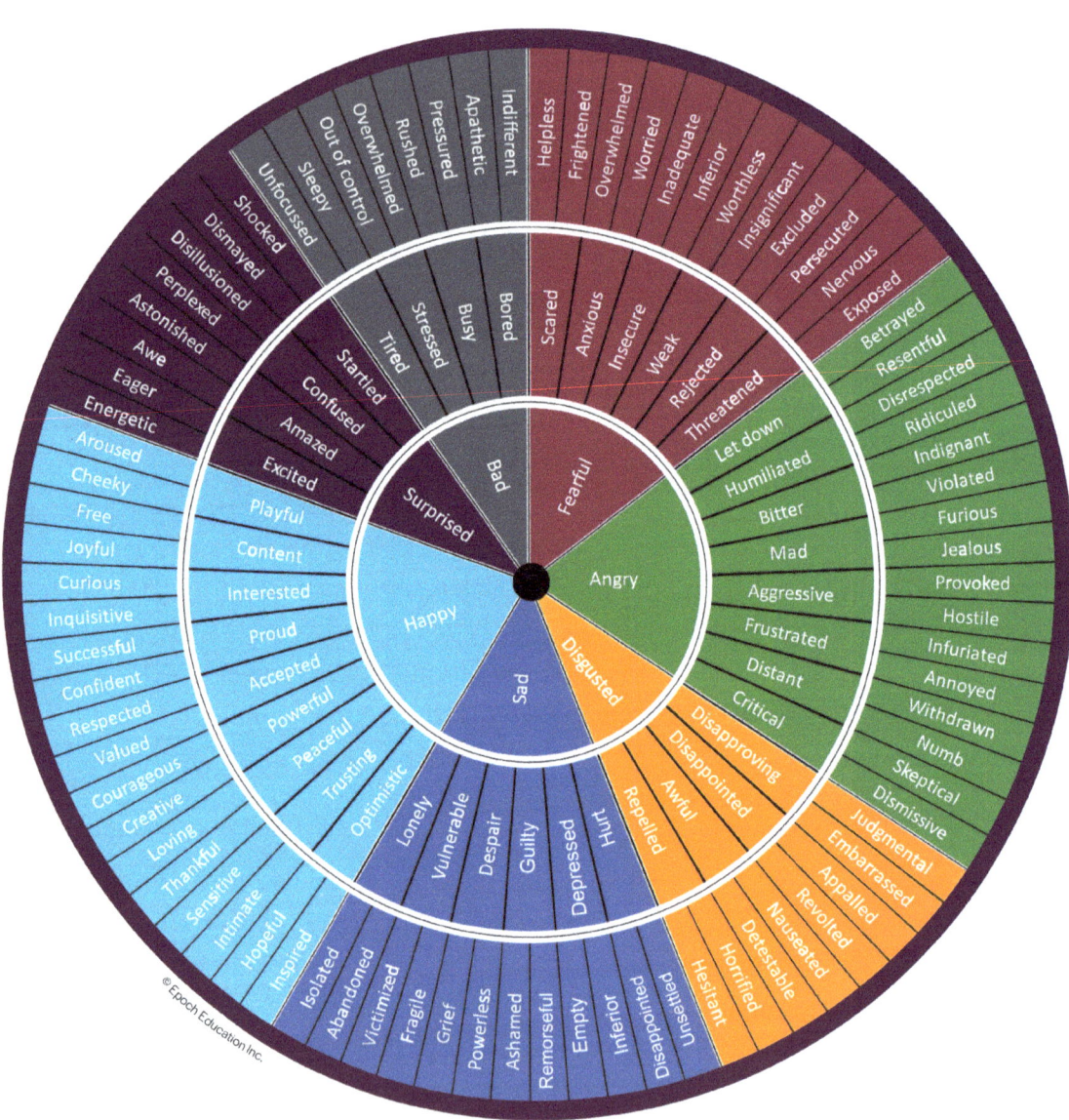

What's Next?

If you've opted to work with a group or partner, you know who those growth partners are and have set aside time to check in with them at various intervals in this book. You've decided on your preferred method of note keeping and have reviewed the terms.

Now what?

It's time to get started! Note that this workbook is divided into modules:

- Module 1: What is Compassionate Dialogue, and Why Am I on this Journey?
- Module 2: Understanding the RIR Protocol
- Module 3: My Intrapersonal Journey and the RIR
- Module 4: My Interpersonal Journey and the RIR
- Module 5: My Organizational Journey and the RIR
- Module 6: What's Next? Compassionate Dialogue and RIR Application and Practice

We'll begin with the big picture—and your first opportunity to put that journal to use.

"My Why" and My Personal Commitment Statement

✎ Before you start your Compassionate Dialogue Journey, take a moment to think about your own thoughts and experiences. Before moving forward, reflect on your "why" for embarking upon this journey in the first place. Using the following prompts as a guide, write your responses in your journal. Then add the commitment statement provided below and sign and date the entry:

- In the past, my communication in difficult moments looked like: _____

- What *hasn't* worked for me in the past when engaging in difficult conversations: _____

- My initial action and reasoning was: _____

- As I reflect, I realize I was: (examples include not compassionate, not empathetic, avoidant, etc.) _____

- When I first Recognized this, I felt: _____

- Next time something like this occurs, I'd like the following impact/result: _____

Now, lets zoom out:

- Have you found yourself in uncomfortable situations where you wish you had better solutions? Explain.
- Why are you doing this work?

I Recognize that I am on a journey, and I am committed to moving through this process and internalizing the lessons to the best of my ability. I see how doing so can be an act of self—care, and I am worthy of such acts. Along the way, I am willing to both challenge myself and give myself grace. _____ *[initial here]*

Use the commitment statement above as a guide to help you express your desire for engaging in this work. You may also choose to write your own commitment statement, if that feels better for you. Either way, we will revisit your commitment statement at the end of our time together.

Module 1: What is Compassionate Dialogue, and Why Am I On This Journey?

"Compassion is for all of us—others and ourselves."

Why are you here? And why now? What is compelling you to take this journey? Did you have an incident at work? Were you profoundly affected by the latest headline, school shooting, natural disaster, display of inequity?

I ask these questions because reflecting on how and why we've arrived here can help inform our efforts moving forward.

And those efforts start with understanding a core concept: What is Compassionate Dialogue, anyway?

A Closer Look at Compassionate Dialogue

You've had a lot of terms come your way in a short amount of time, so let's revisit our definition.

Compassionate Dialogue is a way to resolve a problem or find a solution through connection and showing empathy for others and ourselves. It is a more humane, kind, and productive way to engage, disagree, heal, grow, solve problems, and move forward. So often, we get blocked by fear—fear of not saying the right thing, fear of retaliation, fear of not having the right information, fear of not knowing enough, or fear of not having the right to speak on a topic. All these barriers get in the way of effectively engaging with one another. Compassionate Dialogue removes those barriers by proposing a new way to approach these conversations—a way that says you don't have to have all the answers. Instead, you simply have to self-reflect, check in, ask questions, and commit to staying engaged.

There's a lot more to it than that, though.

Compassionate Dialogue is powerful for many reasons, not the least of which is this: the person (or people) with whom you're communicating don't have to know it for it to be effective, making it a very practical form of self-care.

Conversations or outcomes may certainly be more productive if everyone is "speaking the same language," sure—but there is beauty in the fact that such a dynamic is not necessary for you to make progress in the interaction (this is the intrapersonal piece that we'll cover soon).

On the whole, Compassionate Dialogue accomplishes the following individually:

- Keeps us **grounded and centered** during difficult conversations. When you're in a charged situation, it's easy to lose focus on the issue at hand and bring up old actions or inactions. Compassionate Dialogue provides a container to keep the conversation on track and a way to help you navigate the situation with self-awareness.
- Helps us **manage our expectations** of others. Seeking to understand someone instead of seeking to change someone helps us manage our expectations of them—and a given situation—in a monumental way. When we eliminate the expectation that whatever we say will have enough of an impact to change

someone's mind and instead proceed with curiosity, not only are we setting ourselves up not to be disappointed, but we can be more at peace with the result of the interaction—whatever that is.

- Gives us our **"Why."** When we choose to interrupt, we know why very specifically because we've slowed down enough to think about it.

- Makes the **"How" more effective**. When you interrupt using Compassionate Dialogue, your "how" is more powerful because you're communicating in a way that is not only self-regulated but that helps you be heard. While it doesn't guarantee that you'll be successful, it does create a discourse where we're at least trying to hear each other and gives us a chance at success and deeper connection.

- Is a form of **self-care**. If you're holding onto something that happened days, months, or even years ago, have you ever thought about what that is doing to your body? If you can still remember it, it is still weighing on you. Compassionate Dialogue allows you to give your body and your soul release in those moments, affording us the room to heal and take better care of ourselves. At the end of the day, being able to have difficult conversations with compassion is one of the best medicines we can prescribe for ourselves.

And the following collectively:

- Builds trust, safety, and belonging within our environments, both of which lead to **sustainability and consistency**. It's no secret that it's easier to have conversations that are comfortable and to communicate when there isn't a problem. What about when neither of those are the case? It is in these situations that connections can be forged if trust and safety are present—both of which Compassionate Dialogue fosters. Compassionate Dialogue helps us build the trust muscle that says, "I am safe in this space. I can trust you, and you can trust me, even though this feels challenging right now." If this belief is a collective and consistent one, it can grow and sustain healthy organizational cultures and personal structures such as families and friend groups.

- Provides opportunities to engage, fail, and learn without being condemned, which can lead to **new approaches**. When you're not worried about shame or retaliation—and when you know there truly are no such things as bad questions—you open the door for so much productivity, growth, and innovation that would have otherwise been stifled. This creates space for new ways of thinking and acting that can lead to new innovative approaches

- Builds empathy and understanding to set boundaries and expectations, which can lead to **collective responsibility**. Communicating with empathy even and especially in the face of a problem allows us to be part of the solution. Often, that solution will involve boundaries and expectations, some of which may apply to a group in order to achieve the best results. There is a problem with equating "racism" as a moral designation rather than a social or historical practice that we have the power to change. When someone does not uphold those boundaries and expectations, you then get to answer one empowering question for yourself: "There is a point where this conversation is no longer going to be effective. Where is that line?"

The Good Person/Bad Person Binary

Part of practicing Compassionate Dialogue is to rid your consciousness of binaries, at least as they relate to human beings. In a binary, there are only two options: Right or Wrong / Black or White / Good or Bad.

The truth, though, is that we are far more complex creatures than that. It's no secret that there is beauty in the in-betweens. We often are quick to extend grace for and a willingness to step into that grayness when it comes to things like art or cultural exploration, but we don't always give ourselves that same permission.

Take, for example, seeing yourself as a "good person." That is, of course, an inherently positive and healthy view.

But what if, in doing so, we—even subconsciously—hold so tightly to that label that it makes us afraid to make a mistake? Afraid to ask a question for fear of saying the wrong thing?

What if, in clinging so tightly to this image of being "good people," we've collectively lost our ability to dance in discomfort and be honest not only about what we know, but what we don't? And, as a byproduct, learn from what that dance teaches us?

Part of being a "good person" is understanding that you might not know the exact right thing to say to every person or the exact right way to handle every situation, but that doesn't take you out of the equation. Instead, those moments in between the binary are invitations to become a better person. To lead, ask, and learn with compassion, curiosity, and courage.

The inverse is true here, too: If someone says or does something that you perceive makes them a "bad person," do you write them off? How "bad" do they have to be before you explode, retreat, or freeze? Sometimes—as we'll discuss in depth when we cover the "Repair" in The RIR Protocol—writing off is what is best . . . but not always. There is so much room for complexity between the good person/bad person binary that we owe it to ourselves, and each other, to explore it a little more in a compassionate way.

✎ When was the last time you avoided having a conversation (or avoided asking a question) out of fear of being perceived as less than a "good person?"

- What happened?
- How did you react, and how did that make you feel?
- When was the last time you thought someone was a "bad person?" What happened?
- How did you react, and how did that make you feel?

Tone and Body Language

We all have different styles of communicating and different affects with which we engage with others based on our circumstances. It is not only our words that convey how we communicate, though. So does our tone and our body language, much of which is unconscious. And while it is helpful for us to understand that we are conveying these messages, it's also important for the receiver to understand that body language and tone don't outweigh the message being conveyed. And sometimes it is incumbent upon the listener to be able to hear with different ears to get to the heart of the matter rather than getting lost in how someone sounds or what their body language is saying. When we choose to focus on tone and body language, we are actually detouring from the real issue. This doesn't mean that we have to like "how" someone is saying something, but it's important for us to understand that they may not have control in that moment. What would it be like to give grace to how that message is coming across and instead focus on the message?

If you're feeling uncomfortable with the way someone is communicating, try expressing that in a way that's productive. For example, you might say, "I'm really trying to hear you right now. It would help if we could turn down the heat a little," (or something similar). Choose a prompt that works for you and lets the other party know you're trying to hear them (without making their compliance feel like a prerequisite for being heard).

Activity: Find Your Equity Avatar

Part of making progress in your Compassionate Dialogue journey is understanding where you're starting from on the equity front, as that is the foundation upon which communities of belonging can be built. This will look different for each of us. For example, some of us have been doing the work to ensure we create belonging and inclusion in our climates and cultures for some time, and others haven't thought of what equity might look like for those who don't look like them. That's okay! What's important is the passion for this work and the willingness to keep learning as we move through it. I say "we" on purpose because I'm still learning as I go, too.

In this activity, I'll ask that you try to put an image or language to where you're at right now in your journey. This is important because it will create a baseline for how we look at growth when we revisit this activity later in the book. As you think about what to choose, give yourself grace and understanding. This might be all new to you, and that's okay. It's also okay to personalize this in a way that is meaningful for you.

For example, the equity avatar that felt most true to me a few years ago was not a picture but a song: "More Than Words" by Extreme. When I heard the lyrics, it spoke to how I felt about equity and the DEI space in general, a space in which I've spent a significant portion of my life: this work should be so *much* more than words. The action is where we connect with ourselves, others, and the world.

Here's a sample response from a Compassionate Dialogue Journeyer who chose to use language as her avatar:

> "There is a hymn that we sing often in our church that starts with the line 'Because I have been given much, I too must give.' This has been a mantra of mine for years now. I recognize that I am one of those blessed people that have been showered with good fortune. I'm beautiful and so have received attention and benefits throughout life that I know are a direct result of just the way I look. I was born into an upper-middle class family with plenty of material goods and have never had to want for anything. I've grown up and raised my kids in one of the wealthiest, most beautiful places in the world. I also have a lot of energy and ability and have been a hard worker, helping others, volunteering at local schools and charities.
>
> About 20 years ago I also realized that I have a higher capacity for this kind of work than others. When my kids were young, their friends were constantly at the house—including one friend of my daughters who did not return the invitation. It would frustrate me that things seemed so 'uneven.' But then, in getting to know this friend's mother better, I learned that having another child in the house was hard for her. It required her to have a lot of mental energy, so she timed it according to when she felt like she could handle it. This was SO far from my experience of the world that I couldn't even fathom that as the reason. We all have different capabilities, and we shouldn't judge others based on what WE have or what WE can do but just accept that most everyone else is trying their best.
>
> I, on the other hand, was capable of more, so it was required of me to DO more.

I can't do much to create better equity in the world, but what I can do is live with a little more grace for those around me and with the assumption that others are trying just as hard as I am. And if I am able, I should do more in order to ease the burdens of others and make their life a little easier. So many people have smoothed the way in my life to make my life easier (grandparents, parents, and husband), that when I can turn around and do that for others, I should!"

As I have continued to grow, so has my avatar. Here is my current equity avatar, to give you another example, which I found via a simple Internet search. **(Remember, while I'm giving you several options to choose from, you only need one equity avatar. Choose the format that speaks to you: a poem, a collage, a story, etc . . . whatever is the best medium to express what you're feeling in the moment when you think about this work.)**

While the following image is widely-shared[1], it means a lot to me:

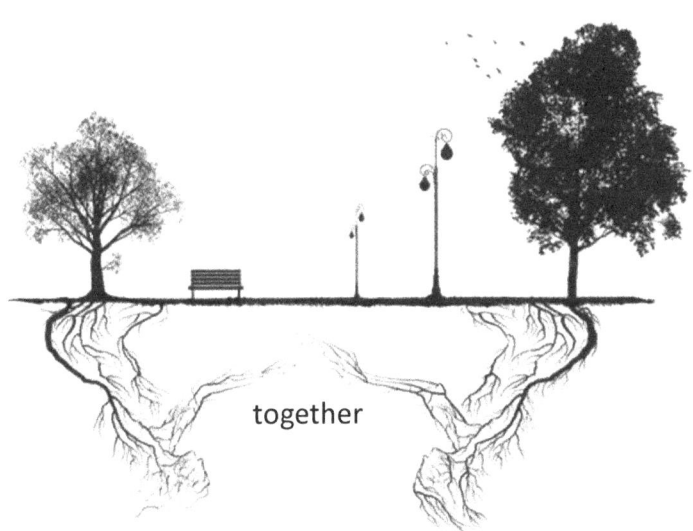

"Like trees who share the same root system, we are but individual expressions of the

---

1. "Can the Wood-Wide Web Really Help Trees Talk to Each Other?" *BBC Science Focus Magazine.* Accessed January 3, 2024. https://www.sciencefocus.com/nature/mycorrhizal-networks-wood-wide-web.

greater whole. When we raise a revolution in our personal psyche, we are serving the quickening of collective consciousness." -DREAMWORK with Toko-pa

My equity avatar has evolved over time and after so many years of doing this work and, sometimes, feeling like it has been an uphill battle, I feel like I have finally come through the other side.

I have found the simple truth that we are ALL connected and interdependent whether we want to believe it or not. So my work now is to demonstrate to the best of my ability, that simple truth."

Please understand that your avatar can evolve. My first avatar (the song) was when I was at the beginning of this work, back when I felt people were paying lip service without putting in real effort. It was two years after the murder of George Floyd, and I was frustrated and disappointed at the lack of action. Today, the tree avatar represents an evolution in my thinking: that there is still a degree of frustration, but I can be part of the solution by fostering connection and belonging. One day, I might go back to the song or choose another avatar altogether. Like ourselves as humans, our relationship to equity is ever-evolving.

Your turn! It's time to meet yourself where you are. Ask yourself honestly: Where are you in your knowledge and ability to navigate issues around equity? What is the difference between equity and equality, in your mind?

✎ In your journal, let's explore that line of questioning a little more:

- What does equity mean to you?
- When have you experienced it? When haven't you?
- When you close your eyes and say the word to yourself, what do you feel?
- When you picture your relationship to equity, what do you see?

Next, do an online search (or browse a magazine or scan your favorite playlist) to find one image or song that speaks to where you are right now in your own personal journey around equity. Maybe you're part of the way down a path, but the road ahead looks long and windy. Maybe it looks clear and safe, like you're almost there. Maybe you find an image of someone holding a sign and marching, or maybe you feel more like a duckling just hatching out of its shell. **Remember, you can also just write and describe your avatar like the sample above . . . whatever resonates with you the most. This is your journey!**

✒ In your journal, cut and paste the image (or describe it) to come back to later. If you chose a song, write the part of the lyrics that most speak to you. Then, describe why this image represents your journey in your typed response. Share this with a friend or colleague, whether they're taking this journey with you or not. We'll come back to this later and see if it still resonates with you or if your image has changed.

Practice & Implementation

Let's revisit Compassionate Dialogue and what it can do for you (and others). It's time to get a little more focused with your reflections and your reasoning for taking this journey.

The following questions are designed to make you think more deeply about not only why you chose to do this work, but also how you think you'll use what you'll learn. Often, calling to mind a real-life scenario helps bring answers to the forefront.

✒ Please answer the following in your journal, and share with any peers who are making this effort alongside you (if you have them):

- In what situations or scenarios do you hope Compassionate Dialogue can help in your life, specifically?
- Is there a situation you can readily call to mind that, upon reflecting, you feel would have ended more productively had you employed a more compassionate approach?

- What value might this bring to your day to day experience of the world, internally?
- What value might this bring to your relationships?
- What value might this bring to your organizations or systems?
- How might this impact how we engage with one another overall?

Module 2: Understanding the RIR Protocol

"The RIR Protocol shows us there is another way. A better way. A more humane, compassionate way to engage, disagree, heal, grow, and move forward."

It's one thing to understand how something works, and it's another altogether to put it into action. Before we move into the nuts and bolts of The RIR Protocol, I want to give you a personal example of how it can look in real life (in this case, my real life).

A while back, I took a weekend road trip with a couple friends. One of those friends—we'll call him James—mentioned we'd be passing through a town where he knew someone. It was one of his old friends from high school whom he hadn't seen in a very long time, so he asked if I minded stopping (as I was driving). I didn't mind, of course.

From the beginning of the visit, I got the feeling that James's friend (who was white) did not appreciate the fact that I am Black. I stayed quiet through a series of microaggressions, **Recognizing** my feelings and thinking about how to, and whether or not to, respond. When the visit was almost over and we were saying our goodbyes, I chose to hug his wife (who was lovely) but not him. As we walked across the street on the way back to the car, he began telling a story about the "Northern War of Aggression."

I'd had enough. I knew it was time to **Interrupt**.

"Is that what you call it?" I asked.

"In the South, that's just what they call it," he said, laughing nervously.

"I am aware of that. I'm asking if that's what you call it?"

He just looked at me and shrugged his shoulders, and I had my answer. I walked back to the car while James said his goodbyes, but I was no longer angry because when I engaged and got my answer, there was nothing else to be done. I knew I had not imagined the microaggressions, which reinforced to me, again, to trust my instincts. Because I'd asked that last clarifying question—something we all too often miss—I knew who this man was. From there, it was my choice as to what the **Repair** would be.

In this case, **Repair** meant I turned to my friend James and said, "We're not stopping there on the way back, if that was the plan."

He was mortified by the situation, agreed, and reinforced that the choice was mine. That is the power of the Protocol in action: it can diffuse your anger quickly so you can move on, and Repair can be as simple as acknowledging and letting go.

Now, let's take a deeper look at each of the components of the Protocol and how they work together.

Recognize

Intentionally pausing while feeling triggered is a muscle you must build. It's challenging, especially at first, because these situations are often emotionally charged and can send us into fight, flight, freeze, fawn, or flock mode. On top of that, all of this happens in a split second!

Without taking the time to **Recognize** its impact on you, your next action may not be the desired one. That's where the **Recognize** portion of the RIR Protocol comes in.

Truly **Recognizing** calls for us to know ourselves, know our triggers, and understand how we react when specific emotions are activated.

For example, when I am angry, I fight and yell . . . and sometimes throw things. When I am sad, I cry. When I am frustrated, I become speechless, and so on.

It is important for me to understand these facts about myself. If a feeling is activated and the **reaction** is not one I want in the long run, then I know I need to ride my emotional wave so that I can **respond** in a compassionate way.

In this section you will have an opportunity to know yourself in a more conscious way; understanding how our identities play a role in how we respond to others and what we choose to respond to.

The Physical, Mental, and Emotional Process of Recognizing

In general, we have been conditioned not to embrace our feelings. When we have a physical reaction to something, our normal tendency is to stuff it down. Hide it. Push it to the back. This is especially true if that feeling is considered "negative."

Consider, though, that both negativity and positivity may be based on someone else's value statement. Emotions and feelings are normal reactions to external stimuli. We (often unconsciously) assign meaning to them based on our lived experiences and societal norms.

That is one reason that the first step in Recognizing is focusing on the body. Why? Because our bodies know something is off before our brains do, and we must learn to look for, decipher, and trust the cues our bodies send us.

For example, if I feel a sensation at the back of my neck, I know I'm unsafe. If I feel a pit forming in my stomach, I know I'm uncomfortable. There is a significant difference between being unsafe and uncomfortable, but if I didn't take the time to understand my body, I may very well confuse the two . . . especially in an emotionally charged moment.

You can get to that level of awareness, too.

Begin by sitting with the triggering thought or statement and resist the urge to push it away.

1. Start internally and *breathe*. Ask yourself:
    a. What is happening in my body?
    b. How do I feel?
    c. What do I think/believe about that feeling?

2. Look externally and *observe*. Ask yourself:
    a. Am I safe? Or am I uncomfortable?
    b. Is this the right time to interrupt? If not, when would be?

✎ You've now done your first full walk through of **Recognize**. What challenges do you foresee? Where do you think your strengths lie? Use your journal to answer these questions.

Interrupt

Say you hear a comment that triggers you, and you understand the importance of pausing to notice where your discomfort manifests physically, allowing you to better pinpoint what emotions are at play.

In other words, you've effectively practiced the first "R" in the RIR: **Recognize**.

Well done! Now what?

The next step is the **Interrupt**—which, for our purposes, does not mean the verbal, reactionary, often-hostile interjection you may be calling to mind. In fact, rather than being reactionary and hostile, Interrupting within the RIR Protocol is intentional and compassionate, by design.

Just because it is intentional and compassionate does not mean it's easy, though. There are many reasons that, as humans, we don't **Interrupt** when our gut tells us we should:

What if we're seen as difficult?

What if the person or group rejects us for speaking up?

What if we just can't think of a witty-enough thing to say to meet the moment?

What if, in saying what we want to say, we're afraid we may be speaking for others and aren't comfortable with that duty?

What if we don't think we're the right person to say something?

What if we don't think we have enough information to comment?

What if we don't want to say the wrong thing and hurt someone's feelings?

What if we're afraid of professional retaliation?

What if we're carrying our own trauma, and bringing up our experience as it relates to the issue feels like just too much?

What if we're so fatigued from interrupting—or from the guilt of not interrupting—in the past that the idea of doing it even one more time feels utterly exhausting?

What if . . .

These are all very valid and human emotions. They're also potential roadblocks. The way to forge ahead in these instances starts, ironically, by looking back at the basics.

Activity: My "Why" For Interrupting

To help overcome these commonly-held hesitations, focus on your "why" for interrupting. In Compassionate Dialogue, the **Interrupt** is born of curiosity and has very clear, focused objectives:

- We interrupt to build trust, safety, and belonging.
- We interrupt to provide opportunities to engage, fail, and learn without being condemned.
- We interrupt to build empathy, understanding, and set boundaries/expectations.

If you do this well, you may find that, while difficult, the conversation can actually deepen the connection and lead to a more collaborative resolution.

For that to happen, though, we must consider that embracing the true meaning of the **Interrupt** requires taking an even closer look at what it does *not do*.

- We *do not* interrupt to prove we're right.
- We *do not* interrupt to change someone.
- We *do not* interrupt in an attempt to get someone to change their mind.
- We *do not* use the interrupt as a weapon, and we never use it to shame or silence others.

Using the information above, think about situations you have been in when you were called to interrupt. What was your "why" for doing so? Did it fall more on the Compassionate Dialogue "do's" or "don'ts" list? Be honest. Remember, there's no binary or judgment here.

 Recount a recent conflict or problem and respond to the following in writing:
- Which side of the dos/donts did your response fall on?
- If you had to do it again, how could you use the **Compassionate Dialogue Interrupt** to do it more effectively, if that's appropriate?

Only when we acknowledge that there is room for us to do and be better can we actually take steps in that direction. And that's why we're here in the first place, right? To move forward. Remember, too, the reasons it's important to come from a place of compassion, which can help guide you when you get stuck: you want to understand, to connect, to build or **Repair** a relationship, to clear the air, to heal.

How To Interrupt

Intention is critical in the **Interrupt**. To avoid (even unconsciously) slipping into one of the less compassionate, less productive intentions we just discussed, ask yourself the following questions before saying *anything* out loud:

- What do I want to know about this situation? What questions will I need to ask to do that? Who will I need to engage with to get that information?
- What impact do I want to share/have in this situation/with this person? When and where would be best to initiate that dialogue?

Once you've answered the above for yourself, choose which strategies and phrases feel authentic[2] to you:

- Ask to clarify meaning
- Ask to understand intent
- Separate the doer from the deed
- Address the impact
- Offer another perspective
- Connect with empathy
- Seek to include
- Acknowledge the speaker

---

2. You do not have to have this list memorized each time you utilize the RIR Protocol, nor do you have to recreate the wheel every time. We suggest choosing a couple strategies and phrases that resonate with you and are easy to remember so that you can call upon them quickly and confidently, should the situation require it. Also, remember, the more you practice, the more natural your **Interrupt** will begin to feel.

Specifically, we recommend the following phrases and sentence stems to facilitate your **Interrupt** and help you invite dialogue, acknowledge the speaker, separate the doer from the deed, and connect with empathy:

To clarify meaning:

- "Tell me more about that. I want to understand."
- "What does that mean to you?"
- "Could you say more about what you mean by that?"
- "How have you come to think that?"
- "I heard you say_____ (paraphrase their comments). Is that correct?"
- "Why is that funny?"

To understand the intent:

- "What has been your experience with _____?"
- "It sounds like you're really frustrated/nervous/angry. What is causing that reaction?"

To address the impact:

- "What you said felt _____ to me. Can we talk about it more?"
- "I need to pause for a moment."
- "How do you think that comment would make someone feel?"
- "How would you feel if someone said that to you?"

To offer another perspective:

- "I've had a different experience with _____."
- "I have a different perspective on _____."

- *"I noticed that you _____ (comment/behavior). I used to do/say that too, but then I learned_____."*
- *"I think that's a stereotype. I've learned that_____."*

We'll practice using these strategies and phrases together later in Module 3 with the Conversation Starter Cards tool.

Repair

Does this talk of Interrupting make you think about an awkward interaction? That relative or friend who always says things that make you cringe? The coworker who you simply can't stand to be around because they make backhanded comments about others? That one time you *really* wanted to say something but didn't, so now you just avoid everyone present in the original interaction?

Take heart: an issue can be resolved, no matter how hard it is. An issue that keeps lingering in your mind weeks or years later is unresolved, no matter how simple it might seem on the surface. Maybe you wish you would have acted or spoken differently. Maybe you wish the way you acted or spoke would have had a different outcome. These things happen to us all! The continued thoughts indicate you're still processing and need some form of **Repair**.

Beyond the immediate benefit of Repairing, there is a sustainability component to this process, too. We cannot stop at Interrupting. We must **Repair** if we want to see and be a part of lasting change.

I know what you're thinking: What, exactly, do I mean when I say "**Repair**" in the context of the RIR Protocol?

Repair calls for us to stay engaged with the person and/or issue and work toward a solution. It does not guarantee a happy ending to the interaction, but it does bring humanity back to the discourse. We can agree to disagree respectfully, and we can understand that we each have lived experiences that have helped create the stories we carry and perpetuate. It also builds our "uncomfortable conversation" muscle and gives us a place from which we can both move on after an interaction.

"Repair It" asks us to:

1. Challenge our preconceptions and prejudices and search for commonalities rather than differences.
2. Be curious about the things that make us different and seek out reputable resources to expand our perspective on things like race, culture, identity, and those who share differing viewpoints.
3. Make amends to those that you may have hurt due to your biased perspectives and actions and take responsibility to shift behavior. Sometimes we are just wrong . . . and that is OK. We are humans having a human experience, so each failure truly can be growth if we approach it as such.

I've been at this for so long that now, when I notice I've said something hurtful, regardless of my intent, I **Interrupt** and **Repair** it immediately. I'll say something like, "You know what? I see you're having a reaction to what I said, and I want to clarify what I meant. It came out wrong."

How to Repair

It can be hard to sit down with someone with whom you disagree and try to have any conversation, let alone a compassionate and productive one.

But that approach is not only possible . . . it is the only way we will be able to move forward.

How, exactly, does it work? Just like with **Recognize** and **Interrupt**, the **Repair** part of the process is actionable and intentional. When considering what the **Repair** might look like for your given situation, consider the following questions before saying anything out loud:

- What boundaries could be developed in order to have a functional, professional relationship with each other?
- What new processes or practices could be implemented?
- What collective learning could happen?
- What support will we need for **Repair**?
- How will you follow—up and communicate what **Repair** could look like?
- When is the best time to have this conversation? In what environment might it be most fruitful?
- What impact do I want to have?

Once you've marinated on the above, consider using this language to start those conversations in practice:

- How about we try to have a fresh start with _____ and be more thoughtful about each other's needs?
- It's reasonable that you want _____ .
- You made a good/valid point about _____ .
- I'm not sure what the solution to _____ is, but I understand that you're dissatisfied about it. We're a good team, let's figure out a solution we can both live with.
- I'm sorry I haven't taken your comment about _____ as seriously as I should have. I understand it's something you're concerned about.
- You've been trying to talk to me about _____ for ages, and I have not been responsive. I shouldn't have avoided you.
- I felt attacked, so I attacked back. But that doesn't get us anywhere.
- I've taken to heart what you said about _____ . I might've seemed defensive then—and I don't necessarily understand your perspective as well as I'd like—but I was listening and would like to keep talking.

- I think we went down the rabbit hole about all the issues that have led up to this moment. Can we try to stay present and start with the issue in front of us?

✎ Even though we've only briefly covered **Repair**, take a moment to reflect on the following:

- What do you think your challenges will be around **Repair**?
- Do you have an idea of what relationships are worth Repairing and which are not? What makes you feel that way?

Receiving the Protocol

In this module, we talk a lot about what the protocol is and how to use it. I would be remiss not to discuss what happens when we *receive* the protocol. (We discuss this in-depth in Module 6, but it's relevant here, too.) It's one thing to be the one who is doing the interrupting, but what happens when YOU get challenged or interrupted? Do you get defensive? Do you get angry? Do you shut down? All of these are normal responses, and it's good practice to put yourself on the receiving end so you can be more cognizant of how someone might be feeling when you're interrupting using the protocol.

Remember, the protocol doesn't guarantee that these feelings won't arise. What it does, through inquiry, is open the door for a deeper conversation. If you're on the receiving end, how will you manage your defensiveness?

Good news: the protocol works for you here, too. **Recognize** how you feel in that moment, then ride your emotional wave. **Interrupt** by asking clarifying questions to seek to understand what you may have done (or not done) as part of your role in the interaction. **Repair** by staying connected and engaged when possible with the person and the situation.

Activity: Receiving the Protocol

Think of a time where someone challenged or interrupted you and you did not respond well. Perhaps you reacted rather than responded or let your feelings control you. (This doesn't mean you were necessarily wrong; it just means you reacted in a way that exacerbated the situation rather than resolved it.)

✎ With this in mind, write your answers to the following:

- What was the issue?
- How did you respond?
- Thinking of Compassionate Dialogue, what could you have done differently to inspire a conversation rather than a conflict?
- How could you return to the person and Repair today? What would you say?

This is good practice for us because there will always be a time where someone feels like we have either wronged them or acted inappropriately. While it may or may not be true, it doesn't change that this is how someone feels/their perspective. When this happens—which it will—we have to be prepared to use the protocol as a tool for compassion and healing.

Putting It All Together

I was a vegetarian for 17 years, and one of my older brothers challenged me on that decision for some time. He hosted Thanksgiving one year and decided to put meat in everything. Every side dish, literally everything. Once I realized the problem and **Recognized** how I felt, I decided to **Interrupt** by asking why there wasn't a single thing I could eat (or why he hadn't let me know ahead of time, so I could bring my own). "Black people aren't vegetarians," he said. Which was usually followed by "they also don't eat sushi!" He could really be a knucklehead.

I was angry and knew it was not going to be a good time for me to say anything, so I went to the store and bought a veggie burger for my dinner. I made my burger, packed my car, and let my brother know that if he could not respect my choices, I needed to leave. So I did.

When I got home, I reached out to him again and let him and the rest of my family know I would not be attending any family events until the family could respect my decisions. I let him know I was prepared to wait it out. There was no point in me yelling or being angry; I simply needed to set the boundaries I was comfortable with. Eventually, they respected my decision (in action if not always in words) and I started attending events again, though I remained pretty annoyed at my brother.

A couple years later, my younger brother passed away, and I was devastated because he and I were the closest. But I also realized at that moment that if it had been any other sibling, it would have been worse because my other relationships were not as healthy. I knew I didn't want to lose the relationship with my older brother, so began the journey of **Repair**. My strategy? *Engage, engage, engage!* We didn't solve the entire issue the first time we talked, but we did open lines of communication that had felt closed for some time. That Thanksgiving incident happened to open the door to a larger **Repair** that, over the years, has involved unpacking deep family memories and childhood experiences. This speaks to a larger point: it's important to note that **Repair** can be an ongoing process; it's not something that only happens once. Instead, it calls for us to strengthen our relationships and to continue to work to strengthen our organizations, even if we're no longer talking about the incident or situation that started the ball rolling. The key to an effective **Repair** is staying engaged.

This example showcases the power of the RIR Protocol: though it hasn't been easy, together, both of us have arrived at a place of being willing to acknowledge conflicts, make amends, and not repeat what doesn't serve our relationship.

What's Next?

So far in your *Compassionate Dialogue Journey*, you've learned what the **RIR Protocol** is. In the following modules, we're going to talk about how to use it intrapersonally (with yourself), interpersonally (with others) and organizationally (within systems and structures). Through these modules, you will continue to deepen your understanding of the RIR Protocol as you practice in real time.

Let's go there together!

Module 3: My Intrapersonal Journey and The RIR

"We need to look at ourselves objectively and admit when we're in that struggle, which may stir up some measures of shame."

Imagine you're sitting around the dinner table with your extended family. It's one of those semi-awkward holiday meals punctuated by clinking glasses and side conversations. (If you have never experienced a meal like this, this scene is a prevalent one in film and television, so draw on that for help envisioning the scenario.)

Then, a relative utters what you just read on the Conversation Starter Card[3] at left—or something else that triggers you.

---

3. Here, and at the beginning of several modules, I've included one of our Conversation Starter Cards—tools for applying The RIR Protocol and Compassionate Dialogue in scenario-specific, real life ways. These statements are designed to stir something in you for a key reason: the power of this work—and critical to your ability to internalize it—is in its *practice*. The cards highlight specific phrases some say and beliefs some hold that not only leave room for Compassionate Dialogue, but often warrant it. The more you familiarize yourself with how to apply The RIR Protocol in these scenarios), the more change you may be able to affect and the more at peace you may be with yourself and others.

Pause.

Instead of first jumping to the "What do you do?" question, we're going to—again—practice by taking a moment to examine the *feeling* stage. This is another exercise in the first "R" in The RIR Protocol: Recognizing. I've included The Feelings Wheel again here to help get you started. Remember, the intrapersonal journey is really a feeling journey.

Your Feeling Journey

Use The Feelings Wheel on the following page to help you write your answers to the following questions:

- How do you feel about what you read on the Conversation Card or another triggering statement you've called to mind? (Identify your own emotions.)
- How do you respond when you feel that way?
- What is the outcome of that response for you?
- What has been the impact of that outcome?
- What beliefs does it bring up for you about the situation or the people perpetrating the situation?

After Recognizing as you just did above, the question we are here to grapple with together becomes *what to do about it.*

Activity: My Racial Experience

I am a Black woman. That informs my racial experience. So, in turn, your race is your racial experience. There! Open and shut case for this activity, right?

Of course not. **The purpose of this activity is that we all see ourselves as racial beings and interrogate what that means in the larger intra- and interpersonal contexts in our lives. In other words, your racial experience is not only about how you see yourself but** more about how the world sees you, impacting your experience *as a racial being* in this world.

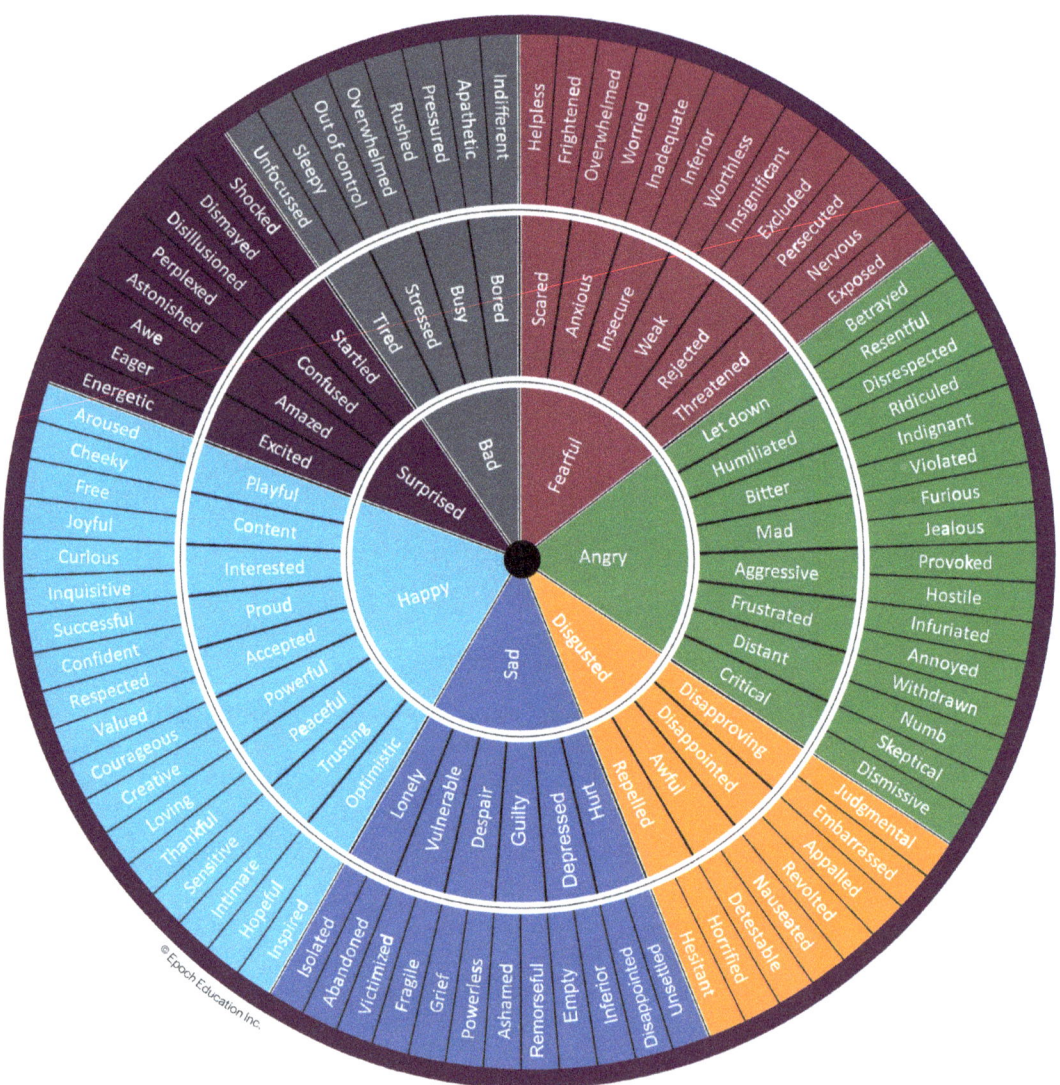

Why is this important? Put simply: race, even as a construct, runs our lives to some extent. And we can't dismantle things we don't understand. Looking at it through this lens helps you understand that you're having a racialized experience whether you believe in the construct of race or not.

For people of color, this helps us talk about the intersectionality of our racial experience, for instance. If someone sees you on the street, they will see you as a person of color. But there is so much more: Are you a person from the south surrounded by people who looked like you? A person who grew up in a diverse environment, like me? None of these are right or wrong. But it's true that both our culture and our cultural experiences influence us. If those around us aren't aware of those parts of our backgrounds, they define us by our race alone. The same can be said for lots of ethnicities. Asians, for example, might be perceived by only that word, not by all the additional cultural implications that accompany being Chinese, Japanese, Vietnamese, and so on. All of these factors play into our racial experience.

Now, let's take a look at not merely what your racial experience is but what it means in the broader scope of your journey.

If you're white, for example, have you ever considered what it *means* to be white? Or Latino? Or Black? Or Asian? What does it mean in terms of how you interact with people? With systems? For example, maybe if you're white, in exploring this line of thinking you decide that part of your racial identity is never having to think about being white. That is not a privilege, for instance, that is part of my racial identity, or those of many others.

Here is an opportunity to revisit your Equity Avatar from Module 1 as you consider your answers to the following questions. Write your responses in your journal.

- When was the first time you noticed differences among others?
- When was the first time you noticed differences in yourself?
- When did you notice you were white/black/etc., for instance? Was it a positive experience or a negative experience?
- Do you Recognize and/or acknowledge the racial experiences of others?
- Do you Recognize your own racial experience?

Activity: My Identity Chart

Outside of race, how do we view ourselves? The following is a brief overview of other factors that contribute to our identities in the world.

I invite you to answer the following prompts. (Note: please do not limit yourself to the characteristics in the list. It is only intended to start your thinking as we begin to reflect on our identities. If you think of another one, add it!) For example, in my journal, next to Religion, I would write: "Spiritual."

Religion	
Thinking Styles	
Ethnicity	
Skills	
Culture	
Education Level	
Nationality	
Income Level	
Social class	
Sexual orientation	
Age	
Gender	
Physical Abilities/Disability	
Body Type	

✒ What came up for you as you identified yourself? Were there categories that you struggled to answer because, well, you never thought about it? Or were you confused as to the "right" answer? Or, did not really know what it was?

The following exercise is going to help you dig a little deeper. It is intended to point out the dissonance between how you see yourself and how others may see you. There are so many ways in which we compartmentalize and are compartmentalized in our experience, and getting that all down on paper can help us process it.

To get started, choose three identities that you feel represent yourself. **Self identities**, specifically, cover how we view ourselves and what defines who we are. I may, for example, choose "woman," "speaker/coach," and "educator." Copy the chart below into your journal, and write your three "self" identities in the left column.

My Identity Chart

Share your 3 "SELF" identities	Share your 3 "OTHER" identities

Now, consider your **other identities**—that is, those characteristics that are also how we view ourselves but that may not be accepted by others. These "other identities" can be the same as our self-identities, but they may also marginalize us. For instance, I could also put "woman" on this list, because there are times I feel that being a woman is to my detriment because my voice isn't always heard in a room that's male-dominated, etc.

✒ Complete the right side of the chart in your journal by listing three marginalized identities. After creating your identity chart, please answer the following prompts in your journal:

- Can you recall an instance when you couldn't show up fully as yourself?

- What do you believe the impact is when you must deny an aspect of yourself?
- How do you feel when you aren't allowed to show up fully?
- What thoughts or feelings come up for you that you may not have considered before as you complete this exercise?

Your Intrapersonal Recognize, Examined

Did the above reflection point give you some discomfort around facing that some of the identities that are core to you are not accepted by others?

I know what you might be thinking: Why would I want to sit with that degree of discomfort when this is supposed to be about self-care? Isn't that counterintuitive?

I understand why you'd have that question. But as Dan Millman said, "The way to control your emotions is to let them flow and then let them go." This feeling journey is a means to an end. If you're willing to sit in the discomfort and understand what it is, where it's coming from, and how it's impacting you, you can ultimately get to a place of resolving it. If you don't, you risk staying stuck.

Let's look at a universal truth: having marginalized identities, visible or invisible, can create a level of discomfort. The path to resolution is increasing our ability to be uncomfortable and notice where we land.

What happens when you normally engage in difficult conversations? Do you freeze? Go numb? Get angry? And if you don't normally engage, why not? What gets in the way of you not engaging?

For a lot of people, this is not understanding the difference between being unsafe and being uncomfortable. When someone attacks our identity—and as long as we're truly safe—we need to feel that we're able to advocate for ourselves. In order to do that, we must be able to sit with discomfort. What does your body tell you about what you're experiencing?

This body focus is important because now that we've Recognized, we have a better understanding of who we are and how we show up. Pay special attention to how you *felt* in your body when deciding what identities to write down, specifically on the right side of the chart. What sensations do you experience? Is that what discomfort feels like for you? Or is it something different? Have you ever let yourself sit with how discomfort *actually* manifests in your body?

It's no coincidence, then, that the first part of interrupting is honing our ability to be uncomfortable.

We're going to practice that now.

Either re-read the card from the beginning of this module, or call to mind your own triggering scenario.

Got it?

Now, take a moment to get quiet and still. Eliminate distractions—no phone, no background noise.

Create silence.

Breathe, and then breathe again. And again. Do not rush this.

✎ In your journal, reflect and write out your responses to the following prompts:

- What do you believe the impact of having a marginalized identity is having on you?
- What did you notice about yourself as you went on your "Feeling Journey?"
- Where did you get stuck or stop?
- What happened in your body?
- What is one thing you can do to ride your "emotional wave" so you can move beyond behavior that might limit you?

Fixed and Growth Mindset: A Deeper Dive

We've discussed the value of paying attention to how emotions manifest in our bodies—i.e., part of Recognizing in the RIR Protocol. Now, it's time to turn our attention to signs and responses that might be less obvious than a goosebump here or a pit-in-the-stomach there. These have to do with our mindset. Understanding our mindset is crucial and directly impacts how we choose to engage with others and the world. Without that self-knowledge, we have no choice but to stay in reaction when interactions get tough.

There has been a wealth of research and writing on the definitions of and differences between a **fixed mindset** and a **growth mindset**. Often, these discussions originate in a professional setting—perhaps, for example, when evaluating how you take feedback or approach challenging projects.

In this exercise, we will use that same lens to examine how a fixed mindset or growth mindset can affect your success (or lack thereof) in using Compassionate Dialogue and the RIR Protocol to communicate more effectively in challenging or emotionally charged situations.

✎ Review the chart below and use your journal to reflect honestly on the questions that follow:

A fixed mindset says:	**A growth mindset says:**
<ul><li>I'm either good at it or I'm not.</li><li>When I'm frustrated, I give up.</li><li>I don't like to be challenged.</li><li>When I fail, I'm not good.</li><li>If you succeed, I feel threatened.</li></ul>	<ul><li>I can learn anything I want.</li><li>When I'm frustrated, I persevere.</li><li>I want to challenge myself.</li><li>When I fail, I learn.</li><li>If you succeed, I'm inspired.</li><li>My efforts & attitude determine everything.</li></ul>

- Do you relate more to the phrases in the left column (fixed mindset) or right column (growth mindset)?
- Note that it's common to oscillate slightly between the two depending on the situation. If this feels true for you, in what scenarios do you find you have a more fixed-oriented mindset, and in what scenarios do you find you have a more growth-oriented mindset?
- What are the differences in those scenarios? (For example, you might be more apt to have a growth mindset in situations or groups in which you feel a high degree of safety and trust.)
- When was the last time you tried to do something close to Interrupt—even without having the language for it at the time—from a *fixed* mindset? What result did you achieve? How did you feel after?
- When was the last time you tried to do something close to our Interrupt—even without having the language for it at the time—from a *growth* mindset? What result did you achieve? How did you feel after?

How do you move from fixed to growth mindset if you feel stuck? The first step is a willingness to admit that you're stuck in the first place. Having consciousness of your own need to change is the foundation for training yourself out of a fixed mindset. This is the spiritual piece of this work; I believe something will show up to challenge you or inspire you to think differently when the time is right. An open-palms approach to our stuck-ness allows us to embrace these moments and make progress.

It's critical to understand here that external influences contribute to our worldview and our beliefs, whether we are aware of them or not. What allows us to ultimately change ourselves, our relationships, and our systems for the better is our willingness and ability to interrogate those beliefs—an act made much more fruitful with a growth mindset.

"Non-Ness" and Unconscious Bias

As we continue to think about our thinking (metacognition) and peel away the layers of our identity, it's important for us to consider what biases we may carry, where we may feel non-ed, or where we may be non-ing other people. Before we move forward, I want to remind you that this isn't about good or bad people; it's about habits and subliminal messages that we've picked up and carried throughout our lifetimes. This is our opportunity to bring them to life so we can unpack them.

Let's start with non-ness. Have you ever considered how much of our language today is insidious, often when we don't realize it? How our words can marginalize people into "non-ness?" How leading with deficits affects how we see others?

Think about it:

Non-white. Non-English speaker. Non-essential worker.

The minimizing tone of these examples illustrates where the "unconscious" part of unconscious bias comes in, which speaks to the value of the intrapersonal part of this work. We've been programmed throughout our lives to believe and think certain ways, without ever stopping to interrogate why we believe and think those things.

When was the last time you confronted a deeply-held belief and asked yourself: *Is this true?*

Probably not often because that, again, is the unconscious piece here. We don't know we need to ask that question.

Until we do—and this is that sign.

This revelation is not meant to feel punitive nor shameful. (Remember, there are no absolutes when it comes to being a "good" person.) We all carry unconscious bias, around language or otherwise. In admitting that, I'm not offering anyone a pass for poor behavior, but rather I am encouraging a higher consciousness that says, "I know why this exists. And it exists, to some degree, in us all."

Only from that place of intrapersonal acknowledgment can we begin to dismantle our own misheld beliefs. Then, we can begin to tackle them in interpersonal and organizational/group scenarios—but again, only if we've done the work ourselves first. By picking up this book, you've committed to doing that work . . . a big step toward progress.

While I know the examples above all start with "non," non-ness encompasses a range of limiting language that is derived from viewing assets as deficits rather than looking at what a person brings to the table. For example, saying "I got gypped" without understanding the historical context doesn't mean anything to anybody. But once you understand that it is correlated with the gypsy people, you begin to understand why this is a slight. Saying "limited English-proficient," for example, instead of "second language learner" focuses on the deficit rather than the strength.

✎ I want to invite you now to think about a time you used language that might have marginalized a person or group—even (and perhaps especially) unconsciously. Even though we're focusing on the external manifestation of your beliefs whether conscious or unconscious, it is important to realize that the statement or issue was a product of your *intra*personal journey. Right now, remember, we're focused on you and how you can Interrupt your own behaviors and beliefs.

- What was the situation?
- What language did you use?
- Did you Recognize your use of non—ness language at the time?
- Upon reflecting, what bias(es) might you have that you didn't know you had before?

The Cycle of Inference

One tool critical to our intrapersonal Recognize is the Cycle of Inference on the following page. By using it, we begin to understand how our thinking can become conditioned if we are not conscious of external influences. It also explains why there are so many differing perspectives. We each bring our lived experiences to each situation, and based on those experiences, we add meaning to what we see. If we are fixed in our thoughts and beliefs, we can continue to reinforce those limiting behaviors by seeking that which resonates to us. However, if we wish to continue to grow, we have to remain open to new information, differing perspectives and ideas, and be willing to change our minds, thus releasing attachments and beliefs that no longer serve us.

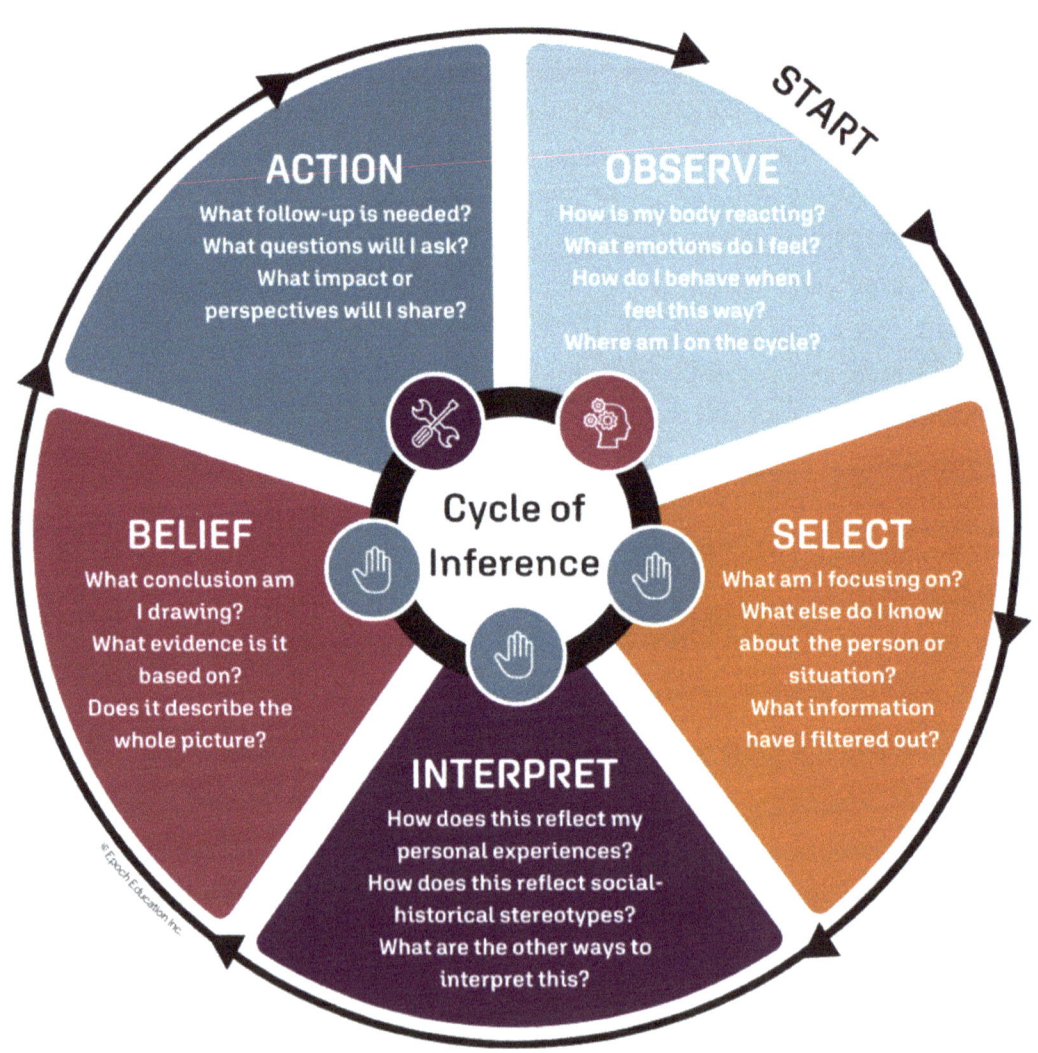

Note that each stage of the Cycle of Inference is accompanied by an icon that signifies whether it is part of Recognize, Interrupt, or Repair. Let's take a look at the cycle in action:

Observe: I had plans to meet a friend for lunch, and she showed up 20 to 30 minutes late.

Opportunity to Recognize:

> What do I feel?

Select: This is the third time she's shown up late to something we've had planned. She didn't apologize, so clearly she doesn't care.

Interpret: This is familiar because I have a history of feeling undervalued.

Conclude: This person doesn't respect my time.

Beliefs: I am not a priority for her.

Actions: When this friend asks me to lunch in the future, I'm going to find an excuse or decline.

The implications of the Cycle of Inference are much more than situational. In the above example, even when I think of this friend outside of the context of trying to set up a time and place to meet, my mind might automatically jump to conclusions or beliefs, thereby reinforcing them.[4]

By using the Cycle of Inference on the intrapersonal level, we begin to identify some patterns and fixed mindsets that we may unknowingly still be carrying or perpetuating. As we bring this to awareness, we become able to use the protocol to Interrupt our own behavior(s) that may be limiting us or impacting how we interact with others.

---

[4] In Module 4, we'll walk through this same scenario using the Cycle of Inference as an interpersonal tool, adding ways to Interrupt.

Your Intrapersonal Interrupt, Examined

I grew up in a unique family situation: there was no adult decision—maker in the house, so my siblings and I had to lie in order to keep up the appearance that there was, indeed, an adult at home. I lied about my age to get a job, lied at school by forging "parent signatures" on forms, etc. This was simply a matter of necessity.

The problem is that the lying continued even after the necessity was over. It became a habit. As I grew older, I found myself lying instinctively, especially if that meant I could avoid an uncomfortable situation. I still knew it was wrong, though. In my twenties, the burden weighed on me. I'd lie reactively and then think, *"Why did I just do that?"* I **Recognized** that my actions were poor and that they sent me into guilt and shame spirals.

What, then, would be my **Interrupt**?

At one point, I decided that the next time I lied unnecessarily, I was going to own it. That was my Interrupt: self-accountability.

After I'd made that promise to myself, I had to keep it relatively quickly. During a phone conversation, I told someone I needed something—but I didn't, really. I certainly wanted it, but the urgency was entirely fabricated because I wanted to get my way. I knew immediately that I needed to hold myself accountable. At that time in my life, I wasn't yet comfortable with picking up the phone and facing that conversation head-on. So, I sat down and wrote a letter. In it, I explained the situation, the impetus for the lie, and apologized for my actions. I dropped it in the mailbox not knowing how it would be received—but that wasn't the point of my Interrupt. It was to right the wrong for *me*. Referring back to the Cycle of Inference, I was able to Interrupt at the select stage because I had already identified the behavior that no longer served me. However, Interrupt can happen at any of the following stages of the cycle (for a visual representation, refer to the Cycle of Inference itself, paying special attention to the icons near the center): select, Interrupt, conclude, belief. There is no right or wrong place to Interrupt; it is fully about when you Recognize and are ready to do so and can vary depending on the situation.

All this is to exhibit that **once we notice behaviors in ourselves that are not congruent with who we believe ourselves to be, who we want to be, or that don't represent us in the light we want to be represented in, we have the ability to change.**

Activity: Exploring Your Own Unconscious Language and Bias (Part 1)

Now it's your turn: call to mind any non-ness language or a belief you carry that you want to look closer at and Interrupt. Ask yourself the following and record in your journal to use to complete this activity:

- What is the scenario you want to unpack?
- What is the feeling that comes up for you when you think about it now?
- What do you want the outcome to be?
- How do you want to feel once this is resolved?

Let's Interrupt:

- Where did this belief stem from?
- What is your relationship to this belief?
- How does this belief serve you or not serve you?
- What question or action can you take to Interrupt this now?

Hold onto this. You're going to have an opportunity to Repair shortly in the second part of this activity.

Your Intrapersonal Repair, Examined

Do you remember that letter I sent in which I apologized for lying? Well, I had no idea how it would be received. When I saw the woman again, I was petrified of what her reaction might be. She walked up to me, gave me a hug, and thanked me for being honest. This was an ideal outcome, surely—but even if it didn't end in this way, my **Repair** would have been the same. It was never about her reaction; it was about me.

This was a watershed moment of understanding in my life. Sending the letter was so uncomfortable that it all but ended my lying completely. I share this story with you not because it's flattering (obviously), but because it's a wonderful example of a core truth of intrapersonal RIR: when we hold ourselves accountable for our actions, good or bad, we can truly begin to shift our behavior. This is obviously an example of a "happy ending," but sometimes **Repair** is divorce. Depending on the interaction, we may decide that this relationship (job, situation, etc) no longer serves us.

This may have been an aha moment for you. It may have been challenging or easy, but at the end of the day, the goal is to Repair what we can in pursuit of greater belonging. What steps are you going to take to ensure you can Repair the language you use or beliefs you carry? Imagine the outcome that you wanted. This is your opportunity to take the steps to reach it.

❀ Activity: Exploring Your Own Unconscious Language and Bias (Part 2)

After reflecting on the questions in Part One, write your own letter . . . to be delivered or not. In it, share what happened and your intention, taking care to note that you understand the impact of your behavior. Also include what Repair you are offering in terms of making amends: Is it sitting and speaking with someone? A promise to be more cognizant in the future? Something else entirely?

Remember, whether you send the letter or not, thinking through Repair at the intrapersonal level is an important piece of this work.

Leveraging the Cycle of Inference allows us to shift our thinking, which ultimately changes our actions and outcomes.

Putting "The Feeling Journey" All Together

We began—and will end—this module discussing not only what we say, think, hear, and believe, but how we *feel* about what we say, think, hear, and believe. This "feeling journey" is directly connected to Compassionate Dialogue and The RIR Protocol because, remember, feeling is how we Recognize. We have also discussed your Interrupt—that is, strategies to "Interrupt" your way of thinking/actions that do not serve you or those around you. Finally, we have begun to unpack what a Repair can look like on the intrapersonal level.

Take a moment to review your responses from the prompts in this module. This will include emotionally-charged language about big topics like race, equity, and identity. Even though they are *your* words and thoughts, if you've answered thoroughly, the weight inherent in your responses will stir something in you, monumental or minute.

Don't push that away. Invite it in.

 Continue to practice by answering the following in your journal:

- What impact has examining your internal beliefs had on how you see yourself? Have they reinforced who you believe yourself to be, or do you see room for growth?
- Is there a follow up/new action that you now want to take to become more congruent with who you say you are or believe yourself to be? Why or why not?
- What strategies will you put in place to hold yourself accountable when you act out of accordance with who you say you are or believe yourself to be?

- How will you continue to extend grace to yourself during the Repair process?

What's Next?

So far in your Compassionate Dialogue Journey, you've learned what the RIR Protocol is and how to use it within yourself as an empowering form of self-care. You might be wondering: *This is so valuable, but I can think of lots of instances where I need a better way to communicate with others, not just in how I handle things solo. Is there a path forward for that?*

There is, indeed. Let's go there together.

Module 4: My Interpersonal Journey and The RIR

"The RIR Protocol allows us to honor each other and meet people where they are, without expectations about where we want them to be."

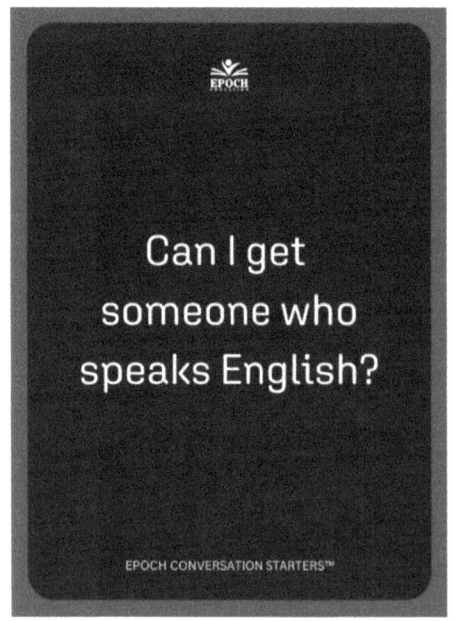

What did you feel when you read the words on the card?

Angry? Validated? Hurt? Satisfied? Confused? Disgusted? Shocked?

The gamut for responses is as varied as we are as people. And those emotions that are under the surface of those are informed by our lived experience. The interpersonal component of the protocol is made for situations like this. It asks, for example: "If you're validated, how do I have a conversation with you if I'm frustrated? More than that . . . Why should I?"

Your Interpersonal Recognize, Examined

First things first, though: for now, simply focus on trying to identify the emotional reaction the card stirred in you, and write that down. (Refer to the Feelings Wheel if you need help!)

(Remember, for this scenario, we're talking about reacting rather than responding. Consider your initial, knee-jerk reaction—not how you would respond using Compassionate Dialogue. Why is this important? Because only when we honestly assess our reactions can we move into our ultimate goal of responding consciously.)

For example, say I feel guilty—specifically guilt tinged with a little bit of embarrassment. When I feel this way, I react by shutting down. The outcome of that response, for me, is that I will disconnect and remove myself from that situation. The impact, then, is that I am ashamed, so I avoid you. Because of that, I form a belief that the relationship is over. I may think, *I just can't get past this shame and guilt, so I can't interact with this person any longer.* This is absolutely not the impact I want . . . which is where the protocol can help.

✎ Now it's your turn, remember that feeling now answer these questions in your journal.

- How do you react when you feel that way?
- What is the outcome of that response for you?
- What has been the impact of that response, so far?
- What beliefs does it bring up for you about the topic or people related to the topic?
- Is the impact you get the impact you want?

The Cycle of Inference: Interpersonal

Once we start building our Intrapersonal Recognize muscle, it impacts how we interact with the world around us. In other words, as our Intrapersonal wheel turns, our Interpersonal one follows by default because they are connected.

The Cycle of Inference exemplifies this larger connectivity. Remember, by using it, we begin to understand how our thinking can become conditioned if we are not conscious of external influences.

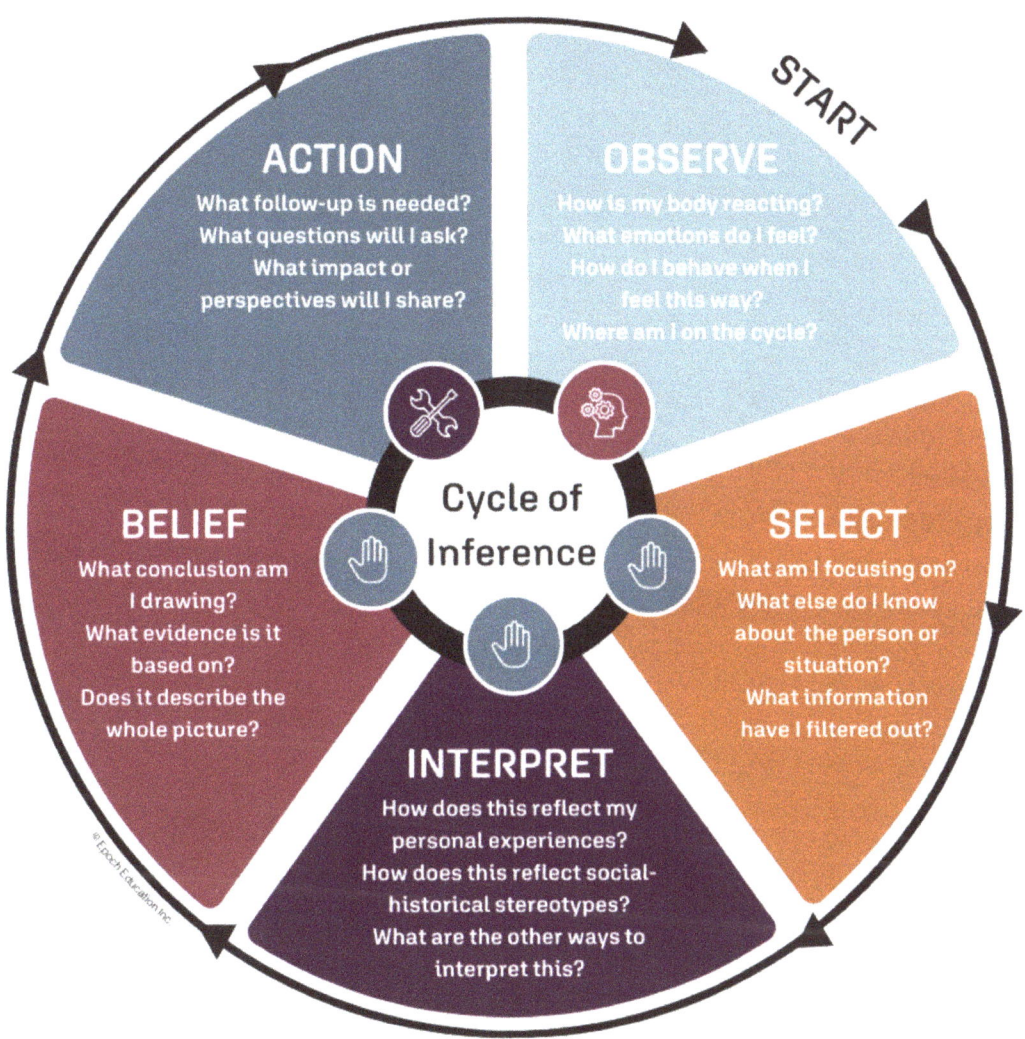

Let's take a look at the cycle in action using the same scenario but focusing on the interpersonal interaction:

Observe: I had plans to meet a friend for lunch, and she showed up 20 to 30 minutes late.

Opportunity to Recognize:

>*What do I feel?*

Select: This is the third time she's shown up late to something we've had planned. She didn't apologize, so clearly she doesn't care.

Opportunity to Interrupt:

>*Ask the question(s) I really want to know: Why are you late? Do you not care?*

Interpret: This is familiar because I have a history of feeling undervalued.

Opportunity to Interrupt:

>*Share the impact of the behavior: When people show up late, I feel undervalued, and I need to share that you showing up late has an impact on me.*

Conclude: This person doesn't respect my time.

Opportunity to Interrupt:

>*Share perspective: When people show up late, it feels like you don't respect my time.*
>*I need to share that with you so that we're clear about how it makes me feel.*

Beliefs: I am not a priority for her.

Opportunity to Interrupt:

>*Share impact or perspective: I feel that you don't value my time when you show up late.*

Actions: When this friend asks me to lunch in the future, I'm going to find an excuse or decline.

Opportunity to Interrupt:
> *Share an action: In the future, when you're late, will you be willing to call and let me know or possibly reschedule if that's a better option?*

In the intrapersonal (Module 3) we Interrupted our thoughts and beliefs. Now, we get to Interrupt our *behavior*, having already mitigated our own feelings and assumptions that may have impacted the way we would have interacted. Notice that we use the same steps in the Cycle of Inference, but the focus is now on how we think about the interaction and ultimately Interrupt through inquiry. This is crucial because through our questioning or sharing of impact, we are able to ascertain the true reason for our friend's tardiness rather than bringing our own luggage to the table.

The implications of the Cycle of Inference are much more than situational. In the above example, even when I think of this friend outside of the context of trying to set up a time and place to meet, my mind might automatically jump to conclusions or beliefs, thereby reinforcing them.

The RIR Protocol shows us another way. For example, next time she invites me somewhere, I might say: "Hey, last time you were late, and I felt a little undervalued. But I'd love to see you at a time that will truly work for you. What do you think?"

Say next time, this friend shows up on time. Using the Cycle of Inference, this is new information for me to observe and select in order to form my beliefs, conclusions, and actions about our relationships. In short, it has helped rewire our relationship. Now, I have the ability to assess my **Repair**. And if she doesn't show up on time the next time, I have the choice to select a different Repair . . . but at least I know which one for sure because I've Interrupted.

Recall how each of the wheels are connected—Intrapersonal, Interpersonal, and Organizational. What we believe impacts how we interact with other people, groups, and systems, which makes the Recognize piece of the RIR so foundational.

🪷 Activity: Assess Your Relationship with the Cycle of Inference

Take a moment to get acquainted with your (likely unconscious, until this point) relationship with the Cycle of Inference in an interpersonal capacity and examine how that's historically played out for you. Answer the following questions:

- When was the last time you made a judgment about a person or a situation?
- How comfortable are you with the idea that you *possibly* might have been wrong or lacked sufficient information to form that judgment? Why?
- What feelings came up for you as you observed the situation?
- What information did you select to reinforce your beliefs?
- Where did those beliefs come from? Are they true? Can you view them through a growth mindset lens that says, "I want to learn" rather than "I want to be right."
- What question(s) could you ask to either confirm or refute your beliefs?
- What question(s) could you ask to be sure you understood the intent behind the interaction?
- What judgment about the person or situation did you make?
- What action did you take, if any?
- What was the result of that action or inaction, on both the situation and for you internally?
- How does the danger of silence/inaction—in situations where action would have been physically and emotionally safe—connect to the difference in fixed and growth mindsets? Be as specific as possible.

Your Interpersonal Interrupt, Examined

What if we could move to Interrupting with the goal of Compassionate Dialogue? What could change, both in terms of your experience of a situation and its potential outcome? Note that your response will depend on who is doing the asking. If it's someone you have a relationship with, for example, your reaction might be different. While still triggered, you might have different energy with someone about whom you care deeply versus with someone you don't know well.

Let's practice some more! Think of a time when you needed to **Interrupt** a racist, sexist, homophobic, or otherwise stereotypical and harmful remark (RSHR).

Do you have a situation in your mind? (If you need help, refer to some of the example conversation starter cards that begin each module—though it is ideal to have a personal situation in mind for this exercise.)

Here are a few examples before we get started:

Statement	How I Could Interrupt
"I think it's weird when Black people acknowledge each other without knowing each other."	"What about that is weird? Can you imagine why that might be happening?"
"Your English is really good!"	"I think you had positive intentions when you said that. However, I feel disrespected because I'm being judged by a stereotype. Can we unpack this a little bit?"
"Girls are such bad drivers. They are always distracted by their phones or looking at their makeup while they're driving."	"I hear your frustration but don't feel as though gender has anything to do with how focused you are as a driver."

✎ Your turn! Using the scenario you called to mind, choose three different statements/questions (or come up with your own). Then, in your journal, describe how you *could have* used each to Interrupt that particular situation with the goal of Compassionate Dialogue.

To clarify meaning:

- *"Tell me more about that. I want to understand."*
- *"What does that mean to you?"*
- *"Could you say more about what you mean by that?"*
- *"How have you come to think that?"*
- *"I heard you say_____ (paraphrase their comments). Is that correct?"*
- *"Why is that funny?"*

To understand the intent:

- *"What has been your experience with _____ ?"*
- *"It sounds like you're really frustrated/nervous/angry........What is causing that reaction?"*

To address the impact:

- *"What you said felt _____ to me. Can we talk about it more?"*
- *"I need to pause for a moment..."*
- *"How do you think that comment would make someone feel?"*
- *"How would you feel if someone said that to you?"*

To offer another perspective:

- *"I've had a different experience with _____."*
- *"I have a different perspective on _____."*
- *"I noticed that you _____ (comment/behavior). I used to do/say that too, but then I learned_____."*
- *"I think that's a stereotype. I've learned that_____."*

For further practice, choose one Epoch Education Conversation Starter card from the graphics below. I invite you to challenge yourself and choose the one that triggers the strongest response in you.

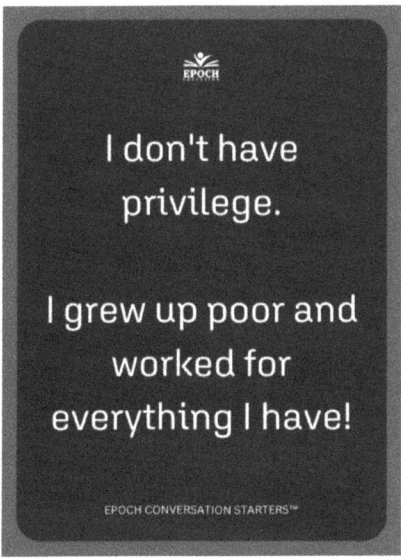 

Using the card you chose, respond to the following questions. RIR reminder cards are on the next page to guide you, should you need help:

- What did you Recognize?
- What is happening in your body?
- How do you feel?
- Why did you choose that card?
- What memories or stories did it trigger?
- How would you Interrupt it using the strategies and questions discussed int his module?
- What could be the impact of that Interruption? Is this the impact you want?

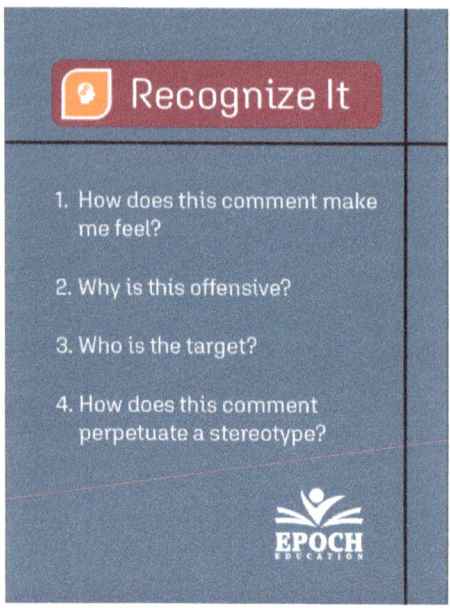
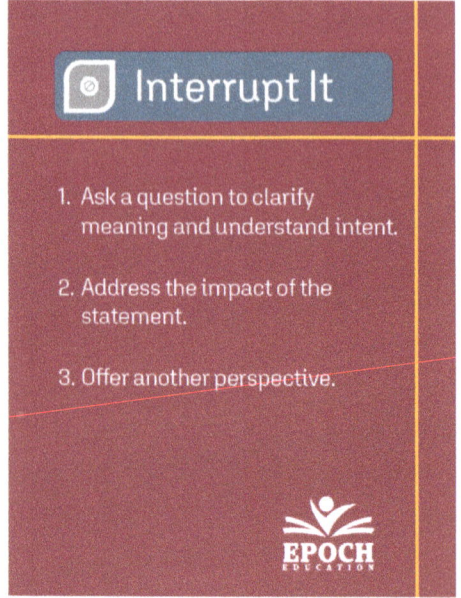
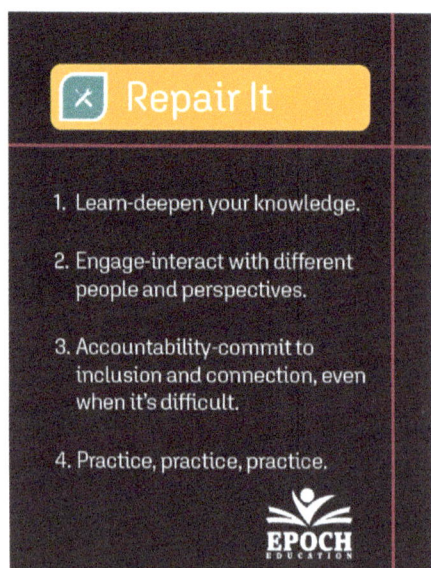

The Conversation Starter Cards are effective because they offer a tangible and repeatable way to build our RIR and Compassionate Dialogue muscles—and they are a wonderful tool to use in practicing with others—something we'll explore next.

✎ For now, take a moment to pause and reflect on a more macro level about the utility of this exercise and how it landed for you:

- Describe how this exercise was for you personally?
- How would you use and apply the Conversation Cards with those you know personally? What do you anticipate to be the outcome(s)?
- How would you use and apply the Conversation Cards with those you know professionally? What do you anticipate to be the outcome(s)?
- How can the Conversation Cards be a tool that you use after you close your Compassionate Dialogue Journey Workbook?

🪷 Activity: Practice, Practice, Practice

Now, let's move back outside of the cards for a moment.

Think about a time when you needed to Interrupt a scenario—a *different* scenario than the one we practiced with above—and describe it in the present tense in three sentences or fewer. The reason? In our earlier exercise, I asked you to consider how you *could have* Interrupted. This scenario is an opportunity to put that practice to use in what would be a new conversation, with the goal of Compassionate Dialogue.

(For example, you might think: There is an important project at the office, and my peers and I are meeting to work on it. As we're getting ready to start, one of my colleagues asks me to take notes to distribute to everyone later. We are all ranked similarly within the organization seniority-wise, and I am the only woman in the meeting.")

Do you have your scenario?

Good!

Next, choose *one* Interrupting statement below that resonates with you (or create your own), and write how you would use it to Interrupt using Compassionate Dialogue. If you're working with a group, share this example with your cohort, and consider role playing to make it feel more real.

To clarify meaning:

- "Tell me more about that. I want to understand."
- "What does that mean to you?"
- "Could you say more about what you mean by that?"
- "How have you come to think that?"
- "I heard you say_____ (paraphrase their comments). Is that correct?"
- "Why is that funny?"

To understand the intent:

- "What has been your experience with _____?"
- "It sounds like you're really frustrated/nervous/angry........What is causing that reaction?"

To address the impact:

- "What you said felt _____ to me. Can we talk about it more?"
- "I need to pause for a moment..."
- "How do you think that comment would make someone feel?"
- "How would you feel if someone said that to you?"

To offer another perspective:

- "I've had a different experience with _____."
- "I have a different perspective on _____."

- "I noticed that you _____ (comment/behavior). I used to do/say that too, but then I learned_____."
- "I think that's a stereotype. I've learned that _____."

Now, answer the following macro questions to reflect on this practice series:

- This new Compassionate Dialogue was _____ for me.
- Interrupting It felt _____ for me.

Your Interpersonal Repair, Examined

If you continue showing up compassionately to conversations, but the other person refuses to give as much as they get, then sometimes that relationship is simply not a worthwhile use of your energy. If, after you've tried to Interrupt and Repair in a relationship—especially if it's been multiple times—that doesn't mean the Repair isn't working.

Instead, it might mean that it *did* work . . . just not in the way you may have thought.

Divorce can be a form of Repair if you've made every attempt but simply can't find a way for the relationship to move forward. In a business environment, for example, rather than letting an employee stay who is not effective and has no desire to change, you let them go. That's a Repair. Conversely, if you're in a situation where you're not respected or valued, it might be time for you to leave. That is also a Repair.

To be very clear here, this is not about merely assimilating a person or being too quick to fire someone/end a personal relationship without trying to make reasonable accommodations. As people committed to communicating compassionately, our goal is to have relationships where we can thrive together and still show up authentically as ourselves.

Through using the protocol, you're trying to create a dynamic that ensures your relationships are spaces for all people, with their unique identities, to not only feel like they belong, but to grow. If someone continues to resist that dynamic after multiple Interruptions, then you know they do not belong in your growth.

Through actively, compassionately engaging and following those processes, you can reach a decision regarding the right time to cut your losses. If you continue Interrupting hurtful behavior and the other parties do not understand and alter course, then they're demonstrating that they are not invested in the relationship or in you.

On the other hand, be sure to leave room for people to make mistakes. I find that we often leave Interruptions one question too soon. If someone says, for example, "I don't care," your next question should be "Why don't you care?" That last question can determine intent and make all the difference in your decision.

Call to mind a relationship in your life that you know you need to address.

Ask yourself:

- What is the benefit to me if I continue this relationship?
- What do I need to happen to continue this relationship in a healthy, nurturing way for myself?
- Is there another question I can ask before I make the decision to end this relationship?
- Is ending this relationship an option? If the answer is no, what actions do I need to take to begin Repair?

Activity: Reflecting on the Big Picture

As we've learned so far together, a lot can be accomplished if we remember to pause at the right moments.

This is one of those moments: let's do a little recap to see how these activities have helped your understanding of Compassionate Dialogue—what it is, how to use it, and what difference it can make in your life.

With your group—or on your own, if you're completing this process solo—answer the following questions:

1. Think of a time you were stuck on a tough decision and/or wanted to challenge a belief. What was the situation, and how did it feel for you, physically and emotionally?

2. Were you able to work through that discomfort? Explain.

3. What do you know now that you didn't know then that might help you do so in the future as you focus on responding, not only reacting?

4. How have you Interrupted biases in yourself and others in the past?

5. What opportunities do you see to improve your processing of—and likely the outcomes surrounding—these in the future?

6. In the scenario you described in Question 1, what could Repair look like using The RIR Protocol? How is that different from the outcome you had?

What's Next?

When you focus on knowing yourself and building strong relationships with others, you cannot help but impact and change organizational climates and systems. Remember, whether it's healthy or unhealthy, everything is connected. When one gear turns, so do the others!

I invite you to think about your organization and groups and the structures within them. Do they invite people in or keep people out? How do people get hired, promoted, and supported in your spaces—and what can you do about it?

Let's go there together.

Module 5: My Organizational Journey and The RIR

"There are actions you can take that can significantly impact an outcome with some thought and intention."

My company works with many organizations and school districts. When we're teaching the latter about The RIR Protocol, we don't always get to work with the school board. (It's often teachers and administrators.)

We soon realized this was problematic because, while the teacher and administrator focus is important and necessary, school board members are often faced with challenging comments at public meetings and aren't prepared to answer questions or engage effectively.

After we made this realization, we made sure to include the school board when working with our next district client. By preparing the school board members to answer questions—and by reminding them that it's not "if" someone is going to challenge them in a public forum, it's "when"—we reduced the risk of them being caught off guard. It took practice, practice, practice! They started meetings, in fact, by pulling a Conversation Starter Card and working through the protocol as a group.

It paid off. The next school board meeting, someone made a public comment that challenged a decision, and the board got to use the protocol. Because they did so well, they were able to respond to a challenging situation in a compassionate, productive way.

This is not purely a tool for education, though. And it's not just for those in leadership roles. It's an opportunity for individuals *in any group* to access and utilize their voices around issues that may be problematic and require attention. The key is that if we are prepared and know the protocol, we can use it to Interrupt marginalizing situations or practices that have been institutionalized or where people intentionally try to thwart the work your organization is trying to do, blocking pathways to creating belonging, equity, and justice.

This works because collectively, by using Compassionate Dialogue within our organizations and groups, we begin to build trust, safety, and belonging. The protocol allows us to honor each other and meet people where they are, without expectations about where we want them to be. We're having an honest dialogue.

When you build that trust, safety, and belonging, you promote sustainability and consistency. I don't have to worry about how we'll communicate with each other when you see me. I don't have to fear abandonment or retaliation if I do something wrong. Together, we establish a new norm. It's sustainable because people feel valued and appreciate that they're being heard. When we are able to contribute at this level within an organization, we can begin to make some real systems change.

As a result of us being heard, we authentically engage with each other knowing that we are striving for a common goal and intentionally allowing different perspectives in our attempt to create a shared understanding and, thus, solution. So many people are unwilling to take risks because they may feel like if they make a mistake or upend the status quo, they'll be condemned when the true goal is finding ways to negotiate these difficult topics and spaces together.

However, if we use the protocol and meet people where they are, we start to create a safe climate and culture that encourages both risk-taking and feedback. We become used to giving and receiving input, which ultimately positively impacts the climate and culture of the organization.

How does this look in practice in our organizations and systems? Let's take a look . . . and (you guessed it) practice a bit.

Your Organizational Recognize, Examined

You might be wondering, *How do I know if my organization (or friend group/family unit/ etc.) has a blind spot . . . if it's a blind spot?*

That's a very good question.

Often, when looking for blind spots, it can help to start by looking for patterns. Are there issues that keep coming up around a topic (for example, hiring and promotion)? A pattern can be a sign of a situation in which the leaders believe a system or structure is fair, but others in the organization might feel as though it's discriminatory.

What then?

The core of Recognizing at the organizational/group level is looking at things—even and perhaps especially the status quo—through an equity lens. It asks: *Are we making sure we're listening to everyone's perspective on the impact of this? I know what I'm feeling, but how might other people be feeling about this?*

When you find a way to bring everyone's opinions and honest experiences to the table, you are more likely to arrive at an Interrupt and Repair that moves the needle toward progress and growth for not only the people within the systems, but the systems themselves.

Mirrors, Windows, and Sliding Glass Doors

When it comes to literature, there are three categories: mirrors, windows, and sliding glass doors—a concept pioneered by well-known children's literature researcher Rudine Sims Bishop[5].

We can also apply this concept outside of books—to where art, culture, organizations, and even bigger questions around equity intersect.

Before we explore that, let's define our terms:

- Mirrors: You see yourself/your identity/your experience reflected
- Windows: You look through and see other worlds—either how they match up or don't match up to your own
- Sliding glass doors: You can both see the other worlds and are able to enter, fostering empathy

✎ Let's start with a basic interpretation of this perspective.

- When you were growing up, did you have books with characters who looked or acted like you?
- Did you see those characters on television, in movies, or even in your peer groups/environments?
- What did it feel like to see yourself (or not see yourself) in these spaces? Did you notice?

There is a common phrase, "You can't be what you can't see." There are certainly

---

5. Bishop, Rudine Simms. *Mirrors, windows, and sliding glass doors* - scenicregional. Accessed June 3, 2023. https://scenicregional.org/wp-content/uploads/2017/08/Mirrors-Windows-and-Sliding-Glass-Doors.pdf.

exceptions to every rule, and I tend to stay away from generalizations. However, in this case, the pain inherent in that statement rings true[6], consciously or unconsciously: What if you never felt represented in the classroom growing up? What if you were one of only a few kids who looked like you in school? What would that experience unconsciously tell you about what you are capable of and deserve, in school and beyond? If you never feel safe to show up fully as yourself, how might that affect you later in life?

These are valid questions and certainly worth asking. Another part of the beauty of Bishop's premise, though, is that it works both ways.

What if you grew up always seeing yourself represented? What if most of your experience with the world was that it was a mirror, and you rarely had experiences or interactions that might be considered windows, let alone glass doors. Even unconsciously, you may gain an exaggerated interpretation of your own self-worth not because of what you're seeing, but because of what you're missing.

Let's extrapolate this concept to institutions and organizations, though we are clear it is equally important in ALL aspects of the workplace as well. People must feel like they belong and believe there is equal opportunity for them to achieve their goals. In order for this to happen, they must see themselves represented in myriad roles to know their goals are achievable.

✎ Ask yourself:

- Based on what you see, who and what do you believe your organization values?
- Think about the processes that exist in your organization. Do they invite all people in or keep some people out?
- How do people get hired, promoted, and supported in your spaces?
- How could you use Compassionate Dialogue to initiate conversations around this idea and affect change?

---

6. Not necessarily the statement as a whole

Your Organizational Interrupt, Examined

Inclusivity helps brands connect on a deeper, more meaningful level with their clients and customers. It also enables them to expand their reach and influence, which promotes business growth and can lead to meaningful **Interrupts**. For instance, Microsoft developed customized controllers for those with physical disabilities in order to make video games less difficult. Nike developed a pro-hijab campaign to bolster representation of Muslim women in the athletic world. While these are large examples, we can learn from them—and our answers to the following questions—to help us think about what we can do better in our professional spaces and in our communities.

Ask yourself: What do your spaces feel like? How do you feel as part of the group? What does your messaging sound like? As an employee in an organization, it helps to have a sense of ownership over these even if you didn't assist in creating them. Consider this: in order for an organization to serve who it's meant to serve, it's got to be willing to listen to the people within it. (And if it doesn't, you can ask yourself if it's a place you need to be. It is imperative that each voice is heard in pursuit of a stronger, healthier organization.)

To help you answer these questions, the following activities encourage you to evaluate how inclusive and diverse your organization is. The first option is corporate and covers brand identity as well as your current marketing assets and channels. The second option is specifically for educational spaces. Choose the tool that makes the most sense to you, and let's get started!

🪷 Activity (Option 1): Equity Walk Through Tool—How Inclusive Is Your Brand/Company?

You do not have to respond to each question. However, please take notes on which areas the business or organization are doing well in and which areas could use additional support/dialogue. Write down your responses . . . it may be eye opening:

- Does the brand's mission, vision, or values use language that emphasizes the importance of diversity, equity, and inclusion?
- Who are the clients/customers? How could they expand the definition of 'target audience' to make it more inclusive and diverse?
- Is the team representative of the people it serves?
- Do they actively research and interview minority groups when developing strategies or campaigns?
- Does the brand seek opportunities to break down stereotypes?

For customer- or client-facing messaging and channels:

- Do the images, photography, and videos they use represent a diverse and inclusive group (sexual orientations, genders, physical abilities, socioeconomic statuses, family structures, races)?
- How do they typically assign roles? For example, are women mostly doing the cleaning?
- Are only heterosexual couples pictured on your website?
- Are they actively looking to circumvent stereotypical roles by showing, not telling?
- Do they use iconography or visual representations associated with a specific culture for purposes that are unintended by the original culture or offensive to that culture?

For written content:

- Do they use language that could be construed as offensive or off-putting to segments of the population?
- Do they artfully co-opt words or phrases unique to ethnicity, culture, or population?
- Do they avoid colloquialisms whenever possible?

- Do they use gender neutral pronouns when/where appropriate?
- Do they use the primary language of the target audience but adjust when possible/necessary?

For digital content:

- In addition to following the guidelines above, are the digital properties optimized for marginalized communities? For example, can people with disabilities use your website without difficulty?
- Have they utilized inclusive design principles, such as readable text, caption options, etc.?

What did you learn? What are you doing well, and where can you grow? How can you have those conversations using Compassionate Dialogue? Write your takeaways as a reflection to this activity.

Activity (Option 2): Equity Audit—How Inclusive Is Your Classroom?

You do not have to respond to each question. However, please take notes on which areas the classroom is doing well in and which area could use additional support/dialogue:[7]

- Do the displays represent diverse cultural materials, photos, words, and art and not simply cartoon representations of diversity?
- Are there positive representations of the racial and cultural identities of students represented in the school?
- Is there high-quality student work displayed and rotated often—work that the students have a say in and have collaborated on?
- Is the climate in the classroom warm and welcoming to all students, meaning

---

7. You can find a rubric for this activity in the Resources section at the end of the book.

the teacher greets students by name and there are joyful learning opportunities present?

- Is the classroom environment conducive to collaborative learning, including flexible seating opportunities that are visible?
- Does the literature in the class library accurately reflect the cultural diversity of those in the class, rather than there being "just a few diverse books?" Do those go beyond biographies and nonfiction?
- Do students feel like they belong in the classroom (that they are known and celebrated as individuals with rich cultural, racial, and intersectional identities) and that the classroom belongs to them (they have confidence with routines and are willing to take leadership roles)?
- Do students have access to the resources to solve problems independently and the support of the teacher, who Recognizes the necessity of the development of their own executive function?
- Are opportunities for independence and autonomy available? In other words, do students know what to do with assignments once they are finished with them, and are classroom activities set up so students can manage their time and behavior?

What did you learn? Where are you doing well, and where can you grow? How can you have those conversations using Compassionate Dialogue? Write your takeaways as a reflection to this activity.

Even if you're not in a classroom or organization, these can spark some questions you might want to ask about your own spaces and with whom you interact within them. (For further practice in identifying your own blind spots, you'll find a Social Media Audit in the resources section at the end of this book.)

Review and Refine Your Approach

✎ In your journal, reflect on your organizational and professional practice in the previous section.

- What came up for you as you used the tool in your physical space?
- What did you observe?
- How will you analyze the evidence to identify trends, strengths, and areas for improvement?
- How can this assist you in engaging in reflective conversations and the Compassionate Dialogue that needs to take place with this information?
- As a result of this activity, list the people who need to be a part of the equity dialogue within the organization.
- How can you encourage this process to become an integral part of the organizational equity process, goals, and plan?
- What will your follow up actions and next steps be?

Your Organizational Repair, Examined

I'd like to remind you once again to give yourself grace as you move through this journey. Did you have some realizations in this module that made you uncomfortable? That's okay—that's why we're here. It won't help to beat yourself up about not coming to these realizations about your workplace, organization, or group sooner. **But once we know better, we are obligated to do better.**

And doing better isn't just good for you as an individual (though that still counts, certainly). Using Compassionate Dialogue on an organizational level has myriad benefits, both in terms of employee satisfaction and the bottom line. Harvard Business Review[8] reports that employees who feel as though they are treated with respect are 63 percent more satisfied with their jobs, leading to increased engagement and retention. In fact, data from Gallup[9] shows highly engaged teams are 21 percent more profitable than those who report low levels of engagement. In that same report, teams scoring in

---
8. "Do Your Employees Feel Respected?" *Harvard Business Review*, June 21, 2018. https://hbr.org/2018/07/do-your-employees-feel-respected.
9. Harter, Jim. "Employee Engagement vs. Employee Satisfaction and Organizational Culture." Gallup.com. Gallup, August 13, 2022. https://www.gallup.com/workplace/236366/right—culture—not—employee—satisfaction.aspx.

the top 20 percent engagement-wise saw a 41 percent reduction in absenteeism and a staggering 59 percent less turnover—all of which contribute to the health of the organization.

Though we're speaking in numbers and statistics here, remember that these numbers and statistics represent real people who, ultimately, play a key role in creating climates and cultures that we endeavor to be equitable. When those real people feel belonging, they have space to grow as human beings *while* doing meaningful work that moves the needle. This two-way-street is indicative of a truly healthy organization.

Activity: Walking Your Organization Through The RIR

That's just a glimpse into the deeper "why." Now, let's take another look at the "how." Before we do that, consider the following questions that will help you with the Repair portion of the protocol that discusses Community Input Mapping. When we think of 'Community' in this context, we are referring to those people who work within the organization (or closely to it) AND are directly impacted by the decision process:

- Who are the community members relevant to the issue?
- How are they impacted?
- Have you heard from them directly regarding the issue?
- What ideas do you have to engage with them directly?
- What power do they have in the system?

Now, I invite you to use the following resource to apply Compassionate Dialogue on a systems-level. Identify an organizational issue at work that you believe needs attention. (For example: hiring, favoritism, unequal discipline, etc.)

- Name it.
- Use the following guidesheet to walk through Organizational RIR.
- Revisit the Community Input Mapping questions above.

THE RIR PROTOCOL – COMPASSIONATE DIALOGUE ORGANIZATIONAL DISCUSSION GUIDESHEET

Having a consistent structure for team discussions, brainstorming, or problem solving helps to build comfort and trust for more open honest dialogue. Using the RIR Protocol framework acknowledges that emotions and beliefs are always present in our group dynamics, and we can build our capacity to engage with different perspectives in **collaboration for the health of our whole community.**

1. Identify the topic/issue the group is discussing.
2. Provide as much information/detail as possible.
3. Use the RIR Protocol to understand initial reactions, make room for clarifying questions/concerns, hear different perspectives, and identify next steps.

RECOGNIZE IT (Self-Regulate)
Observe Yourself: What is your initial reaction to the topic/issue?
- How is my body reacting?
- What emotions do I feel?
- What is my initial story?
- What previous experiences are informing my reaction?

INTERRUPT IT (Dig Deeper)
Approaches:
- Open to other perspectives
- Look for both challenges and possibilities
- Have a growth mindset about change

Dialogue Prompts:
- What general questions or concerns do you have?
- What possibilities do you see?
- Why is this issue important to the organization?
- What is your personal experience with this issue? What has worked? What hasn't?
- How could this be supported by work that is already happening?
- What would need to be created to address the topic/issue?

REPAIR IT (Stay Engaged)
Community Accountability:
- What additional information is needed? Who is responsible for it? What is the timeline?
- What additional conversations are needed? Who should be involved? What is the timeline?
- What is the implementation ask?
- What supports do you need?

© Epoch Education, Inc.

🖋 Take a moment to reflect on the process you just walked through. What did you learn? How could it impact how it addresses issues in the future?

What's Next?

You've just taken a deep dive into Organizational RIR. Here, Repair is specifically and especially crucial for healing and having successful interactions. That said, it's also the step in RIR that you can forget or fail to do when you're emotionally triggered. The tricky part about Organizational Repair is that you can't plan it before you've Interrupted, as the Interrupt outcome will play a part in what your healing—i.e., Repair—looks like. The Repair could be as simple as reengaging or as complex as taking strides toward dismantling practices that have been in place for many years. This could include actions like clarifying expectations and setting healthy boundaries to move forward. Only when you're committed to the Repair can you make progress toward your end result: justice for all stakeholders so that you can be a part of the creation of a climate and culture in which everyone can thrive.

We've come a long way on this Compassionate Dialogue Journey. In our next and final module, we'll further explore how you can apply and practice these tools in your life, personally and professionally.

Let's go there together.

Module 6: What's Next? Compassionate Dialogue and RIR Application and Practice

"Bridge the divide between learning it and living it."

First, take a moment to give yourself credit for moving through these activities and journaling opportunities for the three spheres of The RIR Protocol: Intrapersonal, Interpersonal, and Organizational. I hope you now have a deeper awareness of not only how they are all connected, but how we can all be connected through Compassionate Dialogue.

In the spirit of deepening our awareness, I'd like to pose another question: What's a label that you have been given that doesn't accurately represent who you are? (For instance, some people would call me "aggressive" because of my presence and my approach to conversations. I wouldn't use that language to describe myself, which means that label feels burdensome and untrue to me.)

What about you? What label are you thinking of for yourself?

You don't have to go straight to the big ones. We've created a hierarchy of what "isms" and "ists" matter most in the social context, many of which can be seen outwardly. However, not all identities are visible, and I encourage you to pull back that curtain. For example, you may be a white male who has the privilege associated with both of those identities, but perhaps you have a cognitive disability. Or a problem with addiction. Or an eating disorder. The point is that in some way, to some degree, you understand what it feels like to be othered.

You may have noticed if you have taken this Compassionate Dialogue Journey in partnership with others that sharing your answers with another person helps you become multi-faceted in each other's eyes. This allows us to deepen our authentic connection with each other and build empathy in the spaces that we don't understand. This is evidenced by the power of Contact Theory—that is, the idea that the more you're in contact with people who are different from you, the more accepting you are of others. Contact Theory says that you need to expressly pursue what might make you uncomfortable and that doing so is your responsibility, not the responsibility of those with the marginalized identity which you don't understand.

Contact Theory in action is powerful. A friend of mine—we'll call him Paul—is a compassionate and intelligent man who struggled deeply after the 9/11 terrorist attacks. He felt fear of the Muslim community and consciously and unconsciously conflated them with terrorism—so much so that he'd legitimately panic if he heard anyone speaking Arabic. He knew it was out of hand when, on an airplane, he overheard two men speaking Arabic and informed the flight attendant that they needed to turn the plane around and let them off. Even though Paul reacted in this way, he was able to **Recognize** that his fears were his and not the fault or responsibility of the men on the plane. Thus, he requested to be let off rather than the men be removed.

This shows tremendous responsibility and ownership of his own biases while also Recognizing that he had some very serious fear associated with the situation.

Though he Recognized that his feelings and beliefs were misplaced, he wasn't able to find an **Interrupt** that stuck—that is, until he began to actively seek out the very people he felt so much fear and anger toward (i.e., Contact Theory). Paul spoke to the leader of a local mosque and met many of its members. With each interaction, he began to **Repair** by slowly rewriting his internal narrative that was affecting his thoughts, beliefs, and actions. While he is not immune to the fear coming up every now and then, he is more connected to the reality and thus much more willing to advocate for why change is necessary.

✎ Your turn! Remember my earlier invitation to choose a label that you have been given that doesn't accurately represent who you are? Let's delve more deeply into that now:

- Take a moment to write out the details about the label.
- How does that label make you feel?
- Using what you have learned thus far, Interrupt it using one of the sentence stems we covered in Module 4 (or one of your own).

Finally, ask yourself an important question: **What would you say to the person who labeled you that could lead to a Compassionate Dialogue?**

For example, I might write:

"Some people call me aggressive because I am a strong communicator and speak directly. This often makes me feel like I'm playing into their stereotyped view of the "angry Black woman." It makes me feel small, and I would rather be seen for who I really am: as a leader. Next time, to respond in the moment to someone making this assumption, I might say:

'Can you tell me more about why you think I'm aggressive? I want to understand.' or 'You may not have had this intention, but what you just said felt hurtful to me. Can we talk about that a little more?'"

As you can see from this example, approaching the conversation with an **Interruption** designed to bring us closer together instead of further apart is the first step for healing not just ourselves, but our relationships with others and with the world around us. Once you've Interrupted, your **Repair** will become clear to you . . . just don't forget to Repair it.

Now it's your turn to write yours. How could you respond to the person who mislabeled you?

Bringing It All Together: Receiving the Protocol

After working through the modules, let's bring what you've learned together and zoom out. Whether intrapersonal, interpersonal, or organizational, your Repair, remember, can only come after Recognize and Interrupt. Why? Because if you jump straight to a solution orientation, often the conversation—and, sometimes, the solution itself—won't be fruitful.

It's important to point out that the examples and scenarios thus far have covered the experience of being an initiator in Compassionate Dialogue, but that's only one side of the coin. As we discussed briefly in Module 2, how do you participate in these conversations and respond effectively? How do you receive the protocol?

The ideal way is compassionately, of course—but that's far easier said than done. In my years of doing this work, I've found that people generally respond well to using the protocol for themselves but get defensive when it is used on them, however warranted. This is understandable, especially when emotions like guilt or shame come up. But just because something is understandable doesn't mean it can't be changed. The idea of receiving the protocol is rooted in the idea that we can prepare ourselves to receive feedback, even when it's hard to hear.

Consider the following scenario: No matter how hard you are trying to communicate in a kind and compassionate manner, someone you care about says, "You hurt MY feelings just then."

What do you do?

Instead of moving into defensiveness, move into grace. Remind yourself that the good/bad binary is a construct and does not exist. Nobody is infallible. By being open to the fact that you might have said or done something hurtful—even and especially unconsciously—you are also open to learning how to better be in relationship with others. To be able to falter and still connect with others is a strength, not a weakness.

If you have the opportunity to come together and role play your own scenario (or the Conversation Cards) in a group, make sure you switch roles so you can practice how to receive Compassionate Dialogue, too.

✒ Here are some prompts to facilitate this exercise. Please answer the ones that speak to you in your journal:

RECOGNIZE IT

- When someone brings a new perspective, questions your perspective or challenges your practice/beliefs around equity, what is your initial feeling? (Identify your own emotions.)
- How do you respond when you feel that way? What is the outcome of that response for you?
- What beliefs does it bring up for you about the situation or the person Interrupting?

INTERRUPT IT

- What strategies will you use to regulate yourself, move through any blocks to your own vulnerability, defensiveness and/or rejection of the engagement? (Pause and breathe, guiding question/phrase, etc.)
- How will you be responsive to what the person is asking or sharing?
- How will you authentically participate in the Interruption to understand more about their perspective?

REPAIR IT

- How will you prepare yourself to actively participate in the Repair?
- What questions will you ask?
- How will you acknowledge what was brought to your attention?
- How will you make amends, if necessary?

✿ Activity: My Compassionate Dialogue Journey Reflection and Portfolio

Unleash your creativity! I invite you to use this portfolio activity to showcase what you have learned in your Compassionate Dialogue Journey—and, if you can, to come together in community with others who are also on this path.

First, take a moment to revisit your Equity Image from Module 1. Do you still feel as though that image reflects where you're at on your journey now? Why or why not?

If it's no longer a strong representation of how you feel, choose another image that feels like a better fit. Place them side-by-side, and pause to Recognize how seeing them feels in your body. What emotions do you feel? Pride? Fear? Both? There are no wrong answers, just opportunities to know ourselves better and keep moving forward.

In addition to your equity image(s), compile any photos, drawings, writing samples, prompt responses, and additional items that speak to what you've gained on this Compassionate Dialogue Journey. If any questions or exercises felt particularly moving, be sure to include those responses.

Your portfolio can be a collage, a video, a written statement—any tangible representation of the work you've done. Like many things worth doing, the beauty in this project is in its process. The outcome can vary, but it should include the following elements at minimum:

Be specific and unique in sharing your journey. Please use the following prompts for this reflection:

- Your WHY for embarking on a Compassionate Dialogue Journey.
- What you plan to do after the completion of your Compassionate Dialogue Journey.
- Who will be impacted by your Compassionate Dialogue and RIR Protocol implementation.
- How you will implement compassionate dialogue and RIR.
- Personal insights and professional growth you have gained during your process.

Your Commitment Statement, Revisited

When we began, you signed a Commitment Statement that detailed your promise to yourself for this work.

🖋 Now, it's time to reflect, revisit, and recommit to this work, using the following prompts that are designed to be the capstone to the Compassionate Dialogue Journey reflection you just completed.

- As I focus on all I have learned and practiced to this point, I will use my understanding to guide others with the RIR Protocol. _____(*Initial*)
- **Intrapersonal**. I will use the Protocol with myself by _____. I will begin by interrogating this bias: _____. (*Initial*)
- **Interpersonal**. I will use the Protocol with others by _____. I will begin by addressing this situation: _____. (*Initial*)
- **Organizational**. I will use the Protocol within my organization or group by _____. I will begin by addressing this challenge: _____. (*Initial*)
- Along the way, I will continue to give myself grace and understand that this is a journey. I am open to constantly learning and evolving as I connect more deeply with myself, others, and organizations and systems in my life. _____(*Initial*)

Sign and date this entry in your journal, and note that a full template for your Final Commitment Statement can be found in the Resources section. Give yourself credit for how far you've come while acknowledging the work left to be done; this dynamic is the core of equity work and of progress.

Share the final product with those who have embarked upon this journey with you. If you were not working as part of a cohort, share it with a friend or family member and discuss what you learned. Though it's not necessary for everyone to know the Compassionate Dialogue framework for it to be effective—which is part of the beauty of it—it *does* make a difference when those with whom we are in relationship speak, or at least understand, the same language.

Before You Go

You've pushed yourself on this Compassionate Dialogue Journey, and I hope you feel empowered to have some of those uncomfortable conversations you may have been carrying in your heart or avoiding. When we move forward with compassion, empathy, and curiosity, we have the best chance to succeed—together.

This is a journey for a reason; it is never a checklist or a destination. You may find that you've come a long way, but now that your level of awareness has increased, there will be more opportunities to learn. How will you keep your momentum? I'm here to help. If you want to deepen your knowledge of this important work, here are a couple of places you can start:

- Gather a trusted group and create a book study over Let's Talk About Race (and Other Hard Things): A Framework for Having Conversations That Build Bridges, Strengthen Relationships, and Set Clear Boundaries.
- Practice the RIR Protocol using our Conversation Starter Cards (or have a brainstorming session and create your own cards).

You will find these resources—and so much more—at DrNancyDome.com. I invite you to join me there, or email me at hello@DrNancyDome.com. Remember, every genuine connection we make and every time we practice compassionate dialogue brings us closer to creating communities of belonging, benefitting us all.

✎ Now, in your last prompted journal entry, I invite you to answer the following when it comes to next steps:

- Intrapersonally: How will you practice deeper self-reflection?
- Interpersonally: How will you practice Compassionate Dialogue?
- Organizationally: How will you collaborate and advocate?

✎ Now, reflect on your Compassionate Dialogue Journey as a whole:

- One thing I am thinking is…
- One thing I am feeling is…
- One thing I will do is…

THE RIR PROTOCOL – COMPASSIONATE DIALOGUE GUIDESHEET

Differences of opinion and conflict are normal parts of group and interpersonal dynamics. Our ability to meet these moments with **clarity, compassion, and accountability** determines the health, inclusiveness, and functionality of our organizations. The RIR Protocol provides a common framework and practice for staying empathetically engaged with each other during difficult discussions in order to address the root cause of an issue.

RECOGNIZE IT (Self-Regulate)
Observe Yourself:
- How is my body reacting?
- What emotions do I feel?
- What is my initial story?

Assess the Situation:
- Am I unsafe or am I uncomfortable?

Decide:
- Is this the right time to interrupt?

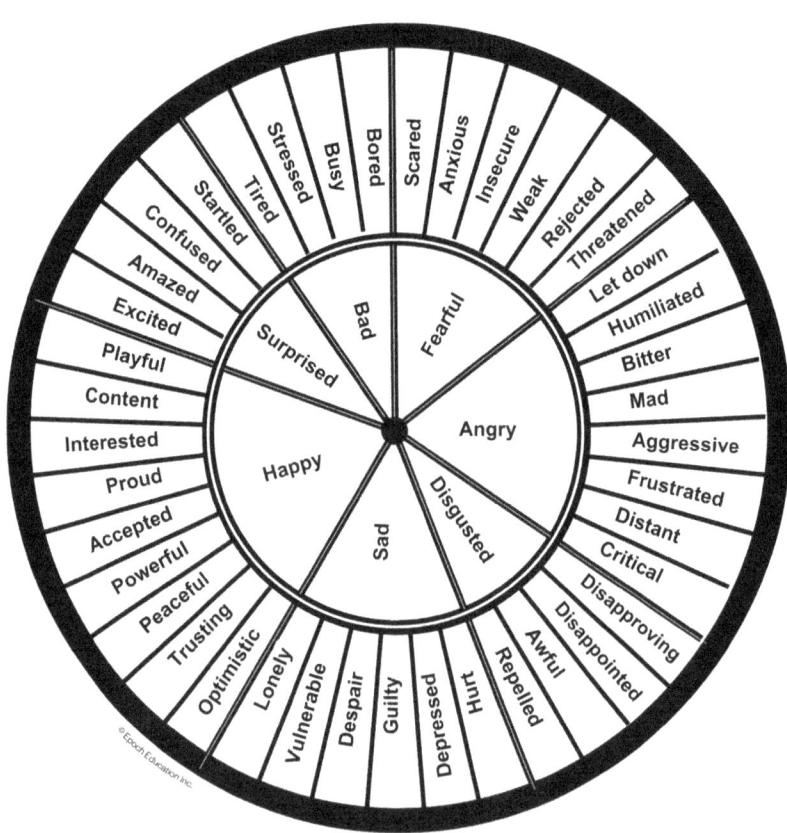

THE RIR PROTOCOL – COMPASSIONATE DIALOGUE GUIDESHEET

 INTERRUPT IT (Dig Deeper)

Approaches:
- Address the behavior.
- Seek the root cause or issue.
- Understand the person you are communicating with.
- Engage in a dialogue.

Strategies:
1. Ask a question to understand the intent, experience, or perspective:
   - "Tell me more about that. I want to understand."
   - "What does that mean to you?"
   - "How have you come to think that?"
   - "I heard you say _____ (paraphrase their comments). Is that correct?"
   - "What has been your experience with _____?"
   - "It sounds like you're frustrated/nervous/angry…What is causing that reaction?"
   - "I don't understand. Why is that funny?"
   - "What are you trying to say/ask right now?"

2. Share the impact, another experience, or perspective:
   - "What you said felt _____ to me and I'd like to talk about it."
   - "I need us to pause for a moment…"
   - "How do you think that comment would make someone feel?"
   - "How would you feel if someone said that to you?"
   - "I've had a different experience with _____."
   - "I have a different perspective on _____."
   - "I noticed that you _____. I used to do/say that too, and I learned _____."
   - "Actually, that is a stereotype…

 REPAIR IT (Stay Engaged)
Create tangible next steps that reinforce mutual respect and accountability.

Take Personal Responsibility:
- Challenge your own biases and preconceptions.
- Engage in your own learning.
- Address your own dialogue diversions.

Re-Connect and Create Accountability:
- Clarify expectations and next steps (interaction boundaries, RIR practice, policy compliance).
- Create a timeline/process for checking back in
- Look for progress.
- Decide if anyone else needs to be involved to support the repair.

© Epoch Education, Inc.

RESOURCES

THE RIR PROTOCOL
CYCLE OF INFERENCE GUIDESHEET

Although our reactions to people and situations can *feel objective*, they are often based on our own *subjective experiences and biases*. The Cycle of Inference shows us the different points in our cognitive process where our biases can surface and potentially impact our decisions and actions.

To help us slow down and create more awareness about our thought process, we can apply the RIR Protocol to 1) Recognize what we observe, 2) Interrupt how we select specific information, make interpretations, draw conclusions, and create beliefs, and 3) Repair by engaging in a Compassionate Dialogue.

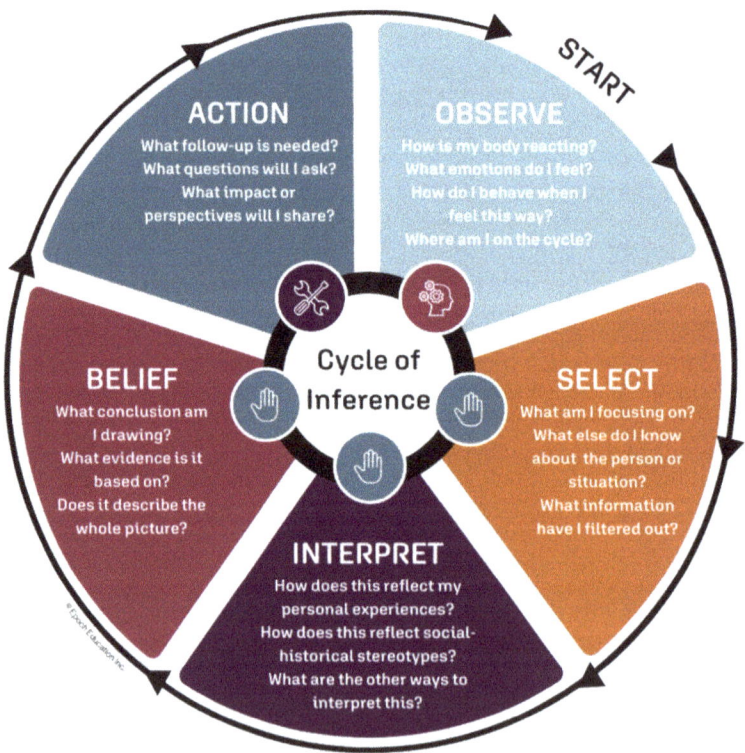

Adapted from Chris Argyris' Ladder of Inference

© Epoch Education, Inc.

THE RIR PROTOCOL
CYCLE OF INFERENCE GUIDESHEET

We can apply the RIR Protocol to the Cycle of Inference to:
- *Debias decision-making*
- *Challenge assumptions*
- *Cultivate growth mindset*

 RECOGNIZE IT (Self-Regulate):
- What is your initial reaction to what you **observed**? What emotions do you have? How do you normally act when you feel this way? What has been the impact of that?
- Where do you automatically jump to on the cycle?

 INTERRUPT IT (Dig Deeper):
- What information did you **select** to focus on? How can you expand your focus? What else do you know about the person or situation?
- What is your **interpretation**? How does it reflect your own personal experiences or perspectives? What are other ways to interpret this?
- What **conclusions** are you drawing? What evidence are they based on? What might you be missing?
- What is your current **belief**? Does it truly describe the whole picture? Does it stereotype or simply who or what you are addressing?

 REPAIR IT (Stay Engaged):
- What **action** will you take to get more information and engage with inquiry and compassion?
  - What questions will you ask?
  - What perspectives will you share?

© Epoch Education, Inc.

THE RIR PROTOCOL – COMPASSIONATE DIALOGUE
ORGANIZATIONAL DISCUSSION GUIDESHEET

Having a consistent structure for team discussions, brainstorming, or problem solving helps to build comfort and trust for more open honest dialogue. Using the RIR Protocol framework acknowledges that emotions and beliefs are always present in our group dynamics, and we can build our capacity to engage with different perspectives in **collaboration for the health of our whole community.**

1. Identify the topic/issue the group is discussing.
2. Provide as much information/detail as possible.
3. Use the RIR Protocol to understand initial reactions, make room for clarifying questions/concerns, hear different perspectives, and identify next steps.

RECOGNIZE IT (Self-Regulate)
Observe Yourself: What is your initial reaction to the topic/issue?
- How is my body reacting?
- What emotions do I feel?
- What is my initial story?
- What previous experiences are informing my reaction?

INTERRUPT IT (Dig Deeper)
Approaches:
- Open to other perspectives
- Look for both challenges and possibilities
- Have a growth mindset about change

Dialogue Prompts:
- What general questions or concerns do you have?
- What possibilities do you see?
- Why is this issue important to the organization?
- What is your personal experience with this issue? What has worked? What hasn't?
- How could this be supported by work that is already happening?
- What would need to be created to address the topic/issue?

REPAIR IT (Stay Engaged)
Community Accountability:
- What additional information is needed? Who is responsible for it? What is the timeline?
- What additional conversations are needed? Who should be involved? What is the timeline?
- What is the implementation ask?
- What supports do you need?

EQUITY WALK THROUGH TOOL

DESCRIPTION

The Equity Walk-Through tool was designed to support businesses in fostering an ongoing lens of cultural responsiveness through a critical examination of their brand. Inclusivity helps brands connect on a deeper, more meaningful level with their clients and customers. It also enables them to expand their reach and influence, which promotes business growth.

SUGGESTED USES

The Equity Walk-Through Tool is designed to help you evaluate how inclusive and diverse your brand identity is, as well as your current marketing assets and channels. This tool is a way to identify opportunities for improvement. It can support shifts in thinking and behavior and encourage reflective practice.

EQUITY WALK THROUGH TOOL

How Inclusive is Your Brand?

Inclusivity helps brands connect on a deeper, more meaningful level with their clients and customers. It also enables them to expand their reach and influence, which promotes business growth. The Epoch Equity Walk-Through Tool is designed to help you evaluate how inclusive and diverse your brand identity is, as well as your current marketing assets and channels. This tool is a way to identify opportunities for improvement.

Brand Identity/Messaging

Consider the following when assessing diversity and inclusion at the Brand Identity/Messaging level:

Does your brand's mission, vision or values use language that emphasizes the importance of diversity, equity, and inclusion?

- Who are your current clients/customers? How could you expand your definition of 'target audience' to make it more inclusive and diverse?
- Is your brand/marketing team representative of the population you serve? Are they a diverse group of people?
- Do you actively research and interview minority groups when developing brand strategies or marketing campaigns?
- Does your messaging address the topics of inclusion and equality, or discuss topics related to diversity and identity?
- Does your brand seek opportunities to address the needs of unique or marginalized populations, or break down stereotypes? (e.g., Microsoft developing customized game controllers for those with physical disabilities or missing limbs making it difficult to play video games with traditional equipment; the Always #Like a Girl campaign, or Nike's Pro Hijab campaign for Muslim women)

EQUITY WALK THROUGH TOOL

Marketing Assets/Channels

Review all customer/client-facing marketing materials or channels (website, print media, social media, presentations, etc.) that you utilize using this checklist. Note where you are doing well; could use improvement; or missing the mark.

Images/illustrations/photographs

- Are always inclusive and diverse; whenever possible and appropriate visuals include a broad representation of ethnicities, gender identities/roles, sexual orientations, physical abilities, family structures, and socioeconomic.

- Consider role assignment and portrayal to ensure the visual is not promoting racist, sexist, ageist, homophobic, or other stereotypes. (e.g., women always doing the cleaning; romance is always heterosexual).

- Actively uses 'non-traditional' role assignment and portrayal to break down stereotypes (a gay couple with their children, a model with a physical disability, etc.).

- Does not use visual representations or iconography associated with a specific culture for purposes that are unintended by the original culture or offensive to that culture's mores.

Written content:

- Does not contain language that may be construed as offensive or off-putting to segments of the population.

- Does not artificially co-opt words or phrases unique to ethnicity or culture population (i.e., verbal/written cultural appropriation).

- Avoids use of colloquialisms whenever possible to promote inclusivity
Uses slang or trending terms with great care and only when appropriate
Uses gender-neutral pronouns when/where appropriate.
- Uses the primary language of the target audience, but always adjusts to in-market language whenever possible.

EQUITY WALK THROUGH TOOL

Digital content (website, social media, blog, community platforms):

- Follows all guidelines above for both written and visual content.

- Is 501-compliant where applicable (i.e., persons with disabilities can use your website without difficulty).

- Uses inclusive design principles (text is readable; images have alt-text and captions; videos are captioned and have transcripts; color contrast is set to 4:5:1; color is not.

EQUITY AUDIT RUBRIC

DESCRIPTION

This rubric was designed to support educators assessing curriculum to maintain an equity lens as they review materials. This Tool can be used for curriculum or literature adoption.

The questions have their roots in Critical Race Theory and focus the user to look for subtle and not-so-subtle details that are regularly absent from reading materials used in schools. It helps keep the user concentrated on ensuring diversity in voice and perspective throughout the process to ensure the materials being adopted are inclusive and comprehensive.

SUGGESTED USES

The tool was initially designed to evaluate textbooks that were being considered for the Social Studies Framework adoption. It can be slightly modified and used for assessing student literature and other written materials across the curriculum.

It would also be a valuable tool to use as a springboard with educators to help expand thinking and create opportunities for open and honest dialogue regarding current practices. It can support shifts in thinking and behavior and encourage reflective practice.

EQUITY AUDIT RUBRIC

Physical Environment: Acknowledgment and Connectedness

Title	Possible Examples	Notes/Recommendations	Rating
1. Displays represent diverse cultural materials, photos, words, art. There are positive, normalized representations of the racial and cultural identities of students represented within the school.	• Wall displays are more than cartoon representations of diversity • Students "see" themselves in the room • Displays recognize contributions of a diverse population		
2. "High quality" student work is displayed.	• Students have a say in the work that is represented on the wall • Examples of collaborative work • Example of progress and growth • Work is fresh, new, rotated		
3. Classroom climate is warm and welcoming to students.	• Teacher greets students individually • Joyful learning opportunities are visible • Classroom "feels" like a place different people want to learn in		
4. Classroom environment is conducive to collaborative learning.	• Flexible groupings opportunities are visible • Flexible seating opportunities are visible • Easy flow and space to move about		
5. Literature (class libraries) reflects the cultural diversity of the students in the class.	• Books are independently accessible to students • Random sampling of books reflect multiple identities		

EQUITY AUDIT RUBRIC

	• There are more than "just a few" diverse books • Diverse literature goes beyond biographies and non-fiction		
6. Students feel like they belong in the classroom and the classroom belongs to them.	• Students are known and celebrated as individuals with rich cultural, racial intersectional identities • Students have confidence with procedures, routines, and expectations • Students take leadership roles		
7. Students problem solve independently.	• Students know where to look to get answers to their questions • Resources are available and easily accessed		
8. Opportunities for independence and autonomy are available.	• Students know what to do when they complete assignments • Activities are set up so students can self-manage their time and behavior		
9. What else did you notice in the space?			

N/A Did not observe 1-absent 2-saw occasionally 3-saw consistently 4-saw outstanding examples of

SOCIAL MEDIA AUDIT ACTIVITY

DESCRIPTION

The Social Media Audit is designed to help us evaluate our inner circle by taking a close look at who is in it and more importantly, who is not. This is an opportunity for us to see where we might be able to grow personally and/or professionally by expanding who we interact with.

SUGGESTED USES

Use this tool to assess how diverse the connections are on your social media channels and to make sure you are not stuck in your personal "echo chamber." You can do this personally or with a team as an icebreaker to begin the conversations around the necessity of diverse networks for achieving equity.

DIRECTIONS

Select one or more social media platforms (Facebook, LinkedIn, Instagram, etc.) that you regularly use to examine who your friends and contacts are, and/or who you're *'following'*. Review your feed/timeline and focus on those who appear most frequently and those whose comments or posts you most frequently interact with (*i.e., those you 'like' or comment on*). As you review your feed/timeline, use the table below to document your observations.

Friends/Contacts/Following Inventory

1. In the left-hand column, record the initials of up to eight people with whom you have a high degree of social media contact or who you follow (do not include family members).

2. Based on what you know about this person, place an X beside those members of your social media circle who are similar to you in each of the following diversity dimensions: gender/sex; nationality; language; age; religion; race/ethnicity.

Initials	Gender	Nationality	Language	Age	Religion	Race/Ethnicity

SOCIAL MEDIA AUDIT ACTIVITY

Reflection Questions

Of the eight people above, how many are similar to you? How many are different from you? Or do you have a mixture of both? Consider the ways in which you are similar or different.

Of the eight people you identified in your social media circle:

- What patterns did you notice?

- How many people from your list match you in 3 or more of your diversity dimensions? Which dimensions?

- How might this influence your perspective or which perspectives you agree/disagree with?

- How does this influence how you view people who are different from you?

Your Final Commitment Statement

- As I focus on all I have learned and practiced to this point, I will use my understanding to guide others with the RIR Protocol. _____(Initial)

- **Intrapersonal**. I will use the Protocol with myself by _____. I will begin by interrogating this bias:_____. (Initial)

- **Interpersonal**. I will use the Protocol with others by _____. I will begin by addressing this situation: _____. (Initial)

- **Organizational**. I will use the Protocol within my organization by _____. I will begin by addressing this challenge: _____. (Initial)

- Along the way, I will continue to give myself grace and understand that this is a journey. I am open to constantly learning and evolving as I connect more deeply with myself, others, and organizations and systems in my life. _____(Initial)

_____
Signature

_____
Date

Acknowledgments

When I think about where I started with the Compassionate Dialogue Journey (CDJ) and where I am today, I am in awe. It was truly a "journey" just to get it written. The original iteration was a far cry from what you've just read. However, without the first drafts, there would be no final draft.

To that end, I would like to start by thanking Shaundra Brown for her initial collaboration when the CDJ was slated to be an online course. Her thoughtfulness and focus on the end user help set the stage for where it would end up. Then there is Debbie Khumayyis who has consistently inspired me to follow where spirit guides me and always encourages me to walk in faith. It was her friendship and support with another completely unrelated activity that unwittingly set the stage for this new, more powerful iteration. She reminds me that practice and reflection support our journey forward and inspired me to get out of my head and into my heart in order to create a journey for the soul rather than solely an intellectual endeavor.

I would be remiss not to acknowledge Jessica Burdg who supported me with my first book and opened the floodgates for everything else that follows. She transitioned from editor to friend and picked up the additional friend duties which consisted largely of patience and encouragement. Thank you for your continued support of my endeavors and your uncanny ability to get in my head to help me tell the story I need to tell.

I would also like to thank the group of educators and friends who went through the pilot and gave valuable feedback to improve the CDJ. Their willingness to fully show up, be vulnerable, and grow together let me know that I had achieved my goal. It is their feedback that helped put the finishing touches on this book. Specifically, thank you to Wendy Neri who, with her literature background, went through each activity as a participant and provided needed clarity and input. Thank you!

I am in perpetual gratitude for Susan Callendar and Kelly Cole, who both allow me the space to create by making sure everything is running smoothly and the business continues to thrive. There are no other people with whom I would rather be in partnership.

Finally, I want to thank my family, my husband Taylor, and my sister Dora for their love and support of my creative process. They are my most consistent fans, and they both, in their own way, hold space for me to be me.

With much appreciation and sincere gratitude,

Dr. Nancy A. Dome

About the Author

Renowned speaker, author, and equity consultant Dr. Nancy A. Dome co-founded Epoch Education in 2014 to provide leaders in education and business with accessible professional development to support equity efforts in pursuit of greater diversity, inclusion, and belonging.

As an educator for nearly three decades, Dr. Dome taught in the Juvenile Court and Community schools. She has worked with our most vulnerable students and has served as a Distinguished Teacher in Residence and faculty member at California State University San Marcos. Dr. Dome consistently strives to be a part of a solution to heal our wounded relationships and improve our ability to effectively collaborate and communicate with one another—as she sincerely believes we are better when we are united.

Her transformative approach helps school districts, educational agencies, and businesses throughout the country and internationally as they navigate complex topics, build bridges, and work together for inclusive, impactful change.

Dr. Dome is the author of the bestselling book *Let's Talk About Race and Other Hard Things: A Framework for Having Conversations That Build Bridges, Strengthen Relationships, and Set Clear Boundaries* that laid the foundation of Compassionate Dialogue as a mainstream strategy to support the development of strong workplace climates and cultures. In 2024, she published this book, *The Compassionate Dialogue Journey: A Workbook for Growth and Self-Discovery*, that provides a pathway for internal exploration by guiding readers through prompts and exercises designed to deepen their Compassionate Dialogue practice as a form of self-care.

When Nancy is not working, she spends much of her time in service to her community, gardening, and making memories with her loved ones.

www.ingramcontent.com/pod-product-compliance
Lightning Source LLC
Chambersburg PA
CBHW042357030426
42337CB00030B/5133